East-West Poetry

A WESTERN POET RESPONDS
TO ISLAMIC TRADITION
IN SONNETS, HYMNS, AND SONGS

by

Martin Bidney

Volume I in the Series: East-West Bridge Builders

Global Academic Publishing
Binghamton University
Binghamton, New York
2010

I dedicate this book to my seven East-West mentors:

Johann Wolfgang von Goethe
(*West-East Divan* 1819)

Adam Mickiewicz
(*Crimean Sonnets* 1826)

Alexander Sergeyevich Pushkin
("Imitations of the Qur'an" 1826)

Mohammed Marmaduke Pickthall
(*The Meaning of the Glorious Koran: An Explanatory Translation* 1930)

Annemarie Schimmel
(*And Muhammad Is His Messenger* 1985)

Karen Armstrong
(*Muhammad: A Biography of the Prophet* 1991)

Katharina Mommsen
(*Goethe und der Islam* 2001)

Bidney, Martin.
  East-west poetry : a western poet responds to Islamic tradition in sonnets, hymns, and songs / by Martin Bidney.
      p. cm. -- (East-West Bridge Builders ; v. 1)
   ISBN 978-1-58684-275-8 (pbk. : alk. paper) 1. Islamic poetry--History and criticism. 2. Literature, Comparative--Islamic and English. 3. Literature, Comparative--English and Islamic.
4. Koran--Appreciation--Poetry. 5. Islam--Appreciation--Poetry.
6. Koran as literature. 7. Islam and poetry. I. Title.
   PJ827.B53 2009
   809.1'938297--dc22
                     2009036052

Published by Global Academic Publishing
Binghamton University, LNG 99
Binghamton, New York 13902-6000 USA
Phone: (607) 777-4495. Fax: (607)777-6132
Email: gap@binghamton.edu
Website: http://academicpublishing.binghamton.edu

Table of Contents

PART 2: LYRICAL RESPONSES TO THE QUR'AN WITH REFERENCE TO OTHER SOURCES

PART 3: LYRICS ON ISLAM-RELATED THEMES

Introduction

I wrote this bridge-building poetry book for everyone: readers of the East and West, Muslims and non-Muslims, the general public and the scholar, people interested in comparative religion and cultural history, global-minded thinkers, poets and musicians and painters and lovers of the arts. My lyrics are meant for whoever may want to experience with me how the lessons, metaphors, and tales of a heartening, enlivening legacy help the learner to reimagine life and literature. It is a pioneering book (and I do not know of any like it), with 140 lyrical responses to Islamic tradition by a poet not raised in Muslim belief. By far the largest number of these are replies to excerpts from the essential Islamic scripture, the Qur'an, itself a vastly rich, though in the West greatly undervalued, treasury of poetic feeling, thought, and image (see poem 131). You will find here sonnets, hymns, and songs; story poems, rhapsodies, and laments. Together, they offer the results of an exhilarating venture into new domains of culture and spirit, the fruits of an exploration.

In its overall form, the book is not a narrative but a collection; rather than read it straight through, you might want to browse and sample. I include 108 lyrical responses to the Qur'an. In the first 75 of these (part 1), I respond to the scripture directly; in the rest (part 2) I get help from precursor interpreters, most notably the medieval Persian poet Rumi. The final section (part 3, 32 poems) offers lyrics about various features of Islam-related tradition.

In the Qur'an-based parts 1 and 2, I begin each poem with an epigraph indicating its Qur'anic source or stimulus. And I've arranged the poems in each of the two parts in the order of the source passages' appearance in the Qur'an. That way, you will get the feeling, in each part, that you're reading a lyrical commentary or companion to the Qur'an. In fact, the Qur'an itself, like my sequences of poems devoted to it in parts 1 and 2, is not a narrative but a collection: the suras or chapters of this scripture are organized in the order of decreasing size, not thematic sequence or plot. (The "titles" of the suras are traditional memory aids indicating a theme or image that appears at some point; they often do not indicate the topic or focus of the chapter.) When writing, my habit was to browse and think and dream over passages I encountered and liked in the Qur'an, as I hope the reader may do with this lyrical companion.

To introduce you to my project here, and to the possibly unfamiliar traditions that give it meaning, I'd like first to offer some background on the Qur'an, looking briefly at its relation to the narratives and teachings of the Hebrew and Christian scriptures, with a focus on new Qur'anic offerings. Then I'll attempt a short introduction to Mevlana Rumi, the Eastern poet who has most greatly aided me as interpreter of Qur'anic legacy. Finally, I will sum up what several Western thought-explorers of the East have contributed to my growth as interpreter of Islam-related readings, and so to the making of this East-West dialogue collection.

What immediately strikes the reader of the Qur'an, and of my commentary lyrics, is how intimately interwoven are the three Abrahamic religions: Judaism, Christianity, and Islam. Fascinated by Qur'anic supplements and additions to earlier scriptural tales, and by the Qur'an's newly introduced narratives about familiar scriptural persons, I have focused on these in my response poems. The Qur'an is regarded as entirely spoken by the One God, Allah (Arabic for "The Lord" or "the God"), in words revealed to Muhammad (c. 570–632 CE), the one Prophet of Islam. "Islam" in Arabic means surrender or being subject to the One God; Allah "expand[s]" the believer's "bosom unto the Surrender" (6:126; poem 13). The Prophet, who had many Jewish and Christian friends and acquaintances, was thoroughly prepared for the elaborate yet strongly centered revelations of Allah by his familiarity with the scriptures of Judaism and Christianity.

So tales from these texts are abundantly and richly retold, and often the Prophet received innovative and stimulating supplements to the tales along with central elements of the traditional narratives that are newly recounted. The suras of the Qur'an may be read with great profit, of course, by persons from all cultural backgrounds. And anyone familar with the Hebrew or Christian scriptures will feel immediately at home, even while being surprised by the varied new materials to which Islamic poets such as Rumi were later to respond with interpretive ardor. This makes perfect sense, for Allah repeatedly and emphatically cites both "Torah" and "Gospel" as "a guidance and a light" to His word (Qur'an 5:44–46; poem 10; 5:110; poem 11; 7:157, poem 16; 48:29; poem 48).

The Qur'an presents the God who said "Let there be light" in Genesis as Himself a vision of resplendent light; the passage is far too beautiful to paraphrase (24:35; poem 32). The Garden of Eden in the Hebrew Bible is recognizable yet transformed in a new Qur'anic "similitude" of promised reward to the faithful with its Biblical four rivers presented as made of water, milk, wine, honey (47:15; poem 47; 16:65–69; poem 26); there are rivers "underneath" the Garden (3:136, poem 7; 13:35, poem 22), and a purified, ethereal wine is served there (37:42–49; poem 103). The Qur'anic Adam names not only the creatures of the earth and air, but the very angels of heaven (2:31–33, poems 2, 3). In the supplemented narrative of Cain and Abel, a raven is sent to teach the murderer how to bury his brother (5:31; poem 135); and the Qur'anic tale further teaches the unforgettable lesson (found also in Jerusalem Talmud Sanhedrin 4:1 [22a]) that the murder of one human being may be likened to the killing of humanity as a whole (5:32; poem 9). The fall of the Tower of Babel becomes in Qur'anic thought not quite the disaster it might appear in diversifying the languages of the world, for Allah thought it wise and valuable that contrasting "nations and tribes" emerge, even as it is good that male and female humans differ (49:13; poem 49).

The tale of Abraham's smashing of his father's idols and then being thrown into a fire and rescued, an incident found in Jewish tradition (*Midrash Bereshit* 38:13) though not in Hebraic scripture, is recounted in the Qur'an. The young rebel leaves the largest idol untouched, so when accused he can ascribe the damage to the big god's hostility to his compeers (21:51–69; poem 95). Sadly, such cleverness only enrages the idolators all the more; they command that he be burnt, but Allah makes the fire into "coolness and peace" for Abraham (21:68–69; poems 85, 95). This beautiful episode of the instant relieving of martyrdom strongly recalls the incident in the Book of Daniel (3:6f) where Nebuchadnezzar puts three men into a "fiery furnace" where they remain not only unscathed but accompanied by an angel in the flames.

The retelling of Joseph's misadventures with the conniving wife of Potiphar is enhanced by an amusing episode: reproached by ladyfriends, the offending seductress frees Joseph temporarily from prison. When the extremely handsome man arrives, the women are so flustered by his beauty that they clumsily cut themselves with their fruit knives, and the temptation undergone by the wife becomes more understandable (12:30–34; poem 20). In different mood, a stirring supplement to the tale of Joseph is the touching narrative in the Qur'an of the miraculous shirt he sends to his father Jacob, whereby the latter's lost power of prophecy can be restored (12:91–96; poem 89).

Mosaic tales are comparable in their recognizability and brilliant Qur'anic additions. The pharaoh's wife not only shows in the Qur'an an admirable compassion for the infant Moses, but is additionally inspired to shun the pharaoh's errors in favor of monotheist belief (66:11, poem 37). The theophanic burning bush is here, yet also a newly introduced wonder: Moses' writhing staff at the fire (27:7–11; poem 35). Moses' ascent of Mt.

Sinai is amplified by an account of the mountain's trembling (7:143; poem 85). The radiant miracle of Moses' shining white hand is unique to Qur'anic narrative (20:22, 28:32; poem 94).

David and Solomon retain their royal glory from the Hebrew writings, but with added attainments in the mastery of all living creatures' languages; so David comprehends the talk of ants and commands armies of birds (27:16–19; poem 36). While developing motifs familiar to us from the psalms of David, the Qur'an tells of the participation of the hills and birds in empathetic hymns when he repents (38:18–21; poem 40). To the mighty works of Solomon are added in the Qur'an great labors carried out by jinns or genies, fiery spirits placed, by the will of Allah, under the king's command (34:12–13; poem 38). As in the Book of Proverbs traditionally ascribed to Solomon, Allah draws pedagogic similitudes from living creatures, as from the birds upheld by air (67:19; poem 57), the wondrousness even of a fly (22:73; poem 98), the weakness of a spider (29:41; poem 100), the harshness of a donkey's bray (31:19; poem 102), or the God-inspired honey-alchemy of a bee (16:68–69; poem 26). Allah puts trees and plants into his proverbial instruction, likening a "goodly saying" to a firm-rooted, fruitful tree with heaven-spreading branches (14:24–25; poem 23). The fruits of the date-palm and vineyard are each an emblem, a "portent for a folk who hear" (16:65–69; poem 26). Every ship kept safe at sea is yet another benign portent (42:32–33; poem 43; 31:31–32; poem 101). Allah teaches in similitudes, "in allegories" (24:35; poem 32).

Qur'anic supplemental stories and newly elaborated themes from the Christian scriptures offer interest and variety. The *mahrib* or alcove in a mosque that traditionally signals the direction leading to the holy city of Mecca is often adorned with an inscription from the Qur'an regarding Allah's protection of Mary in her secluded chamber prior to the annunciation, where He supplied her with gifts of food, to the surprise of her guardian Zachariah (3:37; poem 6). The Muslim worshiper is encouraged to think of the prayer alcove as analogous to Mary's chamber and to compare the roles and attitudes of both humble servants or suppliants of Allah — Mary and today's worshiper. In giving birth to Jesus, Mary, hungering and athirst, is miraculously nourished by a rivulet suddenly appearing, a palm tree offering ripe dates (19:23–26; poem 93).

From the Gospels we are familiar with young Jesus teaching at the Temple "as one having authority, and not as the scribes" (Matt. 7:29; Mark 1:22), but the Qur'anic Jesus offers an impressive brief sermon while yet in the cradle (5:110; poem 11; 19:27–34; poem 30). It may be useful to note that although the Qur'an does not consider Jesus a deity, it clearly teaches that his mother was a virgin (19:19–22). In a manner recalling that of the prophet Elisha, who breathed life into a dead child (2 Kings 4:35), Jesus models a bird out of clay and breathes on it; and by Allah's permission it flies (5:110; poems 11, 80). While the crucifixion is not mentioned in the Qur'an, the nativity and youth of Jesus are presented reverently and with love. As we will shortly see, Muslim poets have created parables about Jesus, and with moral lessons he would have admired.

In the domain of moral thought, the Qur'an builds on themes from the Torah and from the Hebraic prophets and books of wisdom as well as offering passages with deep affinities to the sayings of Jesus. The celebrated pronouncement of Allah that "There is no compulsion in religion" (2:256; poem 5) is wholly in accord with the fundamental premise in the story of Adam and Eve: freedom is our birthright, inseparable from our humanity, which will always be subject to error as well as capable of glory. The Mosaic directive to honor one's father and mother (Ex. 20:12, Deut. 5:16) is touchingly observed in a prayer that Muhammad is told to say for his parents (17:23–24; poem 29). Not only Mosaic law but the Mosaic striving for spiritual fullness, even prophetic rapture, finds elaboration in the Qur'an. Moses cries out, "[W]ould God that all the Lord's people were prophets, and that the Lord would put his spirit upon them!" (Num. 11:29); and the Qur'an declares, "Lo! those who ward off (evil), when a glamour from the devil troubleth them, they do but remember (Allah's guidance) and behold them seers!" (7:201; poem 18).

Jeremiah and Isaiah would feel a deep empathy in reading Allah's urging that we come to the aid of orphans and children in need (4:9–10; poem 8); it is crucial to "pay the poor-due" (7:156; poem 16), to show generosity to "the beggar and the outcast" (51:15–19; poem 50). Allah's reproof of those who would proudly be seen at public prayer yet "refuse small kindnesses" to orphans and the needy recalls the tone of Isaiah's teaching (102:1–7; Is. 58:5–10; poem 107). Isaiah would rejoice to hear Allah's command that we "feed with food the needy wretch, the orphan and the prisoner" (76:8; poem 60); to perform this duty is the "ascent" we are each called upon to make (90:8–17; poem 64).

The Prophet himself is likened to a destitute wanderer, an orphan, whom Allah had rescued and nourished (93:1–11; poem 66). Muhammad is therefore counseled never to despair as the prophet Jonah had done (68:47–52; poem 58). The brevity of earthly life and the concomitant need to keep focused on our soul-duties, a teaching that informs the book of Ecclesiastes (Eccl. 12:8–14), is powerfully underscored by Allah (23: 109–114; poem 31). The time to act, to "work," to "do good works," is now (6:136; poem 14; 103:1–3;

poem 105); reliance on prospective deathbed repentance is discouraged (63:9–10; poem 56). The adage that "A soft answer turneth away wrath" (Prov. 15:1) finds a noble expansion in Qur'anic teaching (25:63–72; poem 33).

Jesus' doctrine of the supreme value of forgiveness (Matt. 18:72) is repeatedly confirmed in the Qur'an, where we are urged to "vie with one another" for Allah's pardon, since patience and forgiveness are of "the steadfast heart of things" (3:133–136, 42:43; poems 7, 86). Patience is allied to pardon; we might often appreciate forgiveness for our impatiently misguided prayers, in which we may be as likely to pray "for evil" as "for good" (17:11; 52:48; poem 28). Like the God of Jesus, Allah removes rancor from the heart (7:43; poem 15); "Keep to Forgiveness," He enjoins His Prophet (7:199; poem 18). We should compete in seeking forgiveness, not in hoarding wealth (57:20–24; poem 55); we are warned against "[R]ivalry in worldly increase" (102:1–8; poem 71). Whoever thinks wealth will immortalize is the consumer consumed (104:1–9; poem 72). Forgiveness is even available to the repentant among the jinns or fiery spirits (46:29–31; 72:14; poem 46).

The saying that a grain of corn must die for it to sprout, implying that a death of self precedes an awakening of soul (John 12:24), is reinforced in Allah's comment on the splitting of the grain and date-stone, and on the bringing forth of life from the dead (6:96; poem 12). Nothing in the Qur'an is more important than Allah's central claim to reanimate or "bring forth" the "dead" (7:57; poem 17). Importantly, while emphasizing the emblematic power of the "sown corn" that rises from humble prostration in God-lent strength, Allah reminds the Prophet and his hearers that the same "likeness" may be found, as well, in the "Torah" and the "Gospel" (48:29; poem 48). Similarly, Jesus' parable about the rich man's difficulty in entering heaven as comparable to that of a camel trying to go through the eye of a needle (Matt. 19:24; Mark 10:25; Luke 18:25) recurs in the Qur'an (7:40–42; poem 84). Luxury tempts to laxity, but the sincere in striving are rewarded, for Allah will "tax not any soul beyond its scope" (7:42; poem 15); we are assured that "With hardship goeth ease" (94:5–6; poem 68). We need never despair as Jonah had done (68:48; poem 58).

The Qur'an also affords new perspectives on Satan, a generalized "adversary" rarely mentioned in Hebrew scripture except for the Book of Job, where he assumes a major role, but later becoming the Devil or Tempter who acquires far greater importance when appearing as Jesus' enemy in all four gospels and with added drama in the Book of Revelation. In the Qur'an Satan is also called Iblis, a name traceable to the Greek *diabolos*, or Devil. When Adam had declared their names to all the angels, they bowed to him in reverence, all save Iblis, who "demurred through pride" (2:31–34, poem 3). Jealousy arises from this pride. Such apparently higher beings as the jinns were made of "essential fire," pure and smokeless, while Adam was molded merely of "black mud altered" (15:26–27; poem 24). Satan or Iblis, proud of his own glorious fire-birth, disdained to pay obeisance to a creature lowly made (7:10–13; poem 83).

In sharp contrast to the jealous narrowness of Satan is the all-encompassing inclusivity of Allah, whose traditional ninety-nine Most Beautiful Names are often recited with the help of prayer beads in rosary-like fashion. (Later Islam would develop the complementary idea of the ninety-nine Most Noble Names of the Prophet [poem 113].) The credal seven-verse initial sura of the Qur'an (comparable in its focused formulation to the "Hear, O Israel" of Judaism or the "Our Father" of Christianity) depicts Allah as at once "the Beneficent, the Merciful" and "Owner of the Day of Judgment" (poem 1). In "Pillars of Islam" (poem 110) I compare the five daily Muslim prayers, as well as the five pillars of Islam, to five fingers of the traditional *ḥamsa* amulet that depicts an open hand with the Eye of Allah at its center (and see last line, poem 58).

With a moving and becoming modesty, the Prophet Muhammad, intent above all on proclaiming the glory of Allah, speaks only briefly and obliquely of his own magnificent deeds, which are far more richly elaborated in extra-Qur'anic *hadith* narratives. It is emphasized in the Qur'an that the Prophet was "unlettered," not a learned scribe (62:2; poems 16, 69). He is not appointed as a supervisor or superintendent of worshipers, but as offering a "Reminder to creation" (68:51–52; poem 58). Crucially, Muhammad is "not at all a warder," but "a remembrancer" (88:21–22; poem 63), calling us to a life of heightened achievement so that we may "journey on from plane to plane" (84:19; poem 61). Though, unlike Jesus, he never claims to be "the bright and morning star" (Rev. 22:16), Muhammad offers the morning star as an emblematic goal of the worthy aspiration he was sent to promulgate (86:1–7; poem 62). Allah sent the Prophet "as a witness and a bringer of good tidings and a warner," "as a summoner unto Allah by his permission, and as a lamp that giveth light" (33:45–46; poem 34).

This is the man who underwent what the Qur'an calls "the Night of Power," which is "better than a thousand months" (97:1–5; poem 70). It was on this night that, as the hadith tradition has it, the unlettered Muhammad miraculously read, in a mountain cave at angel Gabriel's urgent behest, from the Qur'an. Since the Prophet had been sent "as a mercy for the peoples" (21:107; poem 96), it was of supreme importance that he accomplish his uniquely God-appointed mission of revealing the Qur'an, even though, doubtful at first of the validity of the request since he could not read, Muhammad had struggled mightily with the relentless Angel in a manner that may recall to us Jacob's wrestling with the divine emissary in the Hebraic narrative. Muhammad's struggle had a far greater consequence than Jacob's: the revelation of a massive scripture to a single Prophet.

Rainer Maria Rilke has interpreted this Night of the Great Recital in "Mohammeds Berufung" or "Mohammed's Calling." I translate Rilke's wonderfully evocative sonnet:

> Into his hiding place upon the height
> What we know well had swiftly happened. He,
> The angel, came — tall, pure, in blazing light.
> All protest waved aside, he pressingly
>
> Asked — tired, bewildered merchant (that is all
> He was), of travel weary, a delay:
> He'd never read before, and now to say
> Such words — a *wise* man would the task appal!
>
> The angel, though, commanded, showed — indeed
> *Again* showed what upon that page was writ —
> Would not give up but urged, insisted: *Read.*
>
> And so he read — so that the angel bowed —
> And was now one who had *recited* it,
> Was able, heard, had done it, was allowed.

The deliberate confusion of personal pronouns in the lyric mirrors the Prophet's terrified bewilderment and, at the same time, his gradual realization that he must conform his will to that of Gabriel, becoming one in mind with him. So it will no longer matter which "he" is thinking, feeling, speaking.

More wonders told of Muhammad enrich Qur'anic lore: visions encountered or, as some say, brought on by the Prophet include the splitting of the moon (54:1–2; poem 52). From a hadith narrative, related movingly in Karen Armstrong's distinguished *Muhammad: A Biography of the Prophet* (Gollancz 1991; repr. Phoenix 2001) 153, we learn of another incident replete with marvels. I recount it in my sonnet "Tranquil Revelation":

> Fostered alike by beauty and by fear:
> Muhammad's kept again within a cave,
> Yet now, with no temptation of the grave;
> Rather, a charmed and an idyllic cheer.

Enemies gathered, and they came quite near
But found him not. A spider spread a vast
Web at the entry. An acacia cast
Her patterned shadows. And a rock-dove clear

Signal of nonintrusion gave: the place
A man would have to set his foot to pass
Into the rock she nested on. With grass

And twigs and eggs she halted hunters' pace.
Like the Night Flight, the tour of planet-spheres,
This grace-rich tale the favored man endears.

Additional hadiths tell more teachings ascribed to the Prophet, for example, that a love of cats is part of the faith (poem 114).

Muhammad's most astonishing exploratory venture was the occasion when, as tradition tells, he went, on the back of the steed Buraq whose name means lightning, from Mecca to Jerusalem, visiting during his journey all the seven planetary spheres. Indeed, the traditional narrative's account of Buraq offers a symbolic image that I, for one, never tire of reimagining (poems 119, 128, 129). But Muhammad tells of this flight only briefly, indirectly (17:1; poems 27, 92), though tradition adds, regarding the lote or jujube tree seen by the Prophet at the "utmost boundary" near the "Garden of Abode," that among its branches are giant angels (53:1–15; poems 51, 138). Regarding the celestial flight of the Prophet, Karen Armstrong claims that it has "entered the Western tradition, because Muslim accounts of the *miraj*, Muhammad's ascent to heaven, affected Dante's account of his imaginative journey through hell, purgatory and heaven in *The Divine Comedy*, even though with typical Western schizophrenia ... he put the Prophet himself in one of the lowest circles of hell" (*Muhammad* 139).

Muhammad, as we learn from a Sahih Bukhari hadith, prepared for this journey through an awe-inducing rite of purification (poem 27). This radical cleansing, achieved when the Prophet's heart was excised, purified, and reinserted in a rite performed by an angel upon a mountain, is referenced in the Qur'an with characteristic brevity when Allah says, "We caused thy bosom to dilate" (94:1–4). In poem 67 I attempt to tell the story with some of the rich detail the hadith narrative accords.

In parts 2 and 3 of *East-West Poetry* I incorporate additional interpretive lore from extra-Qur'anic sources. I have been influenced by Islamic cultural figures such as Hallaj (poem 83), Rabi'a of Basra (poems 126, 137), Turkish cleric and comic folk hero Nasreddin Hodja (poems 95, 102, 122), and

Omar Khayyám in the Edward FitzGerald translation (poems 94, 103), as well as by Western poets William Blake (poems 98, 100) and Christopher Smart (poem 114). But my chief Muslim informant, collocutor, and consultant in Qur'an interpretation is Maulana (later, when he settled in Turkey, called Mevlana) Rumi, a thirteenth-century Sufi bard extraordinary in productivity and depth, and founder of the devotional rites of Mevlevi whirling dervishes. I visited Rumi's green-towered mausoleum in Konia (poem 115) and think of it often, recalling the low-toned Mevlevi flute as I return in reverie: you will hear that flute in my lyrics (poems 80, 87). Rumi, a singer of genius in the mystical Sufi tradition of Islam, is an invaluable tributary to the great sea of Qur'an-inspired poetic depth and splendor; his chief contribution is to have added to Qur'anic themes two vivid symbols: enlivening fire, ecstatic dance.

Fire imagery in the Qur'an is mostly related to sin and punishment (4:9–10; poem 8; 102:5–8; poem 71; 104:4–9; poem 72), even though the fiery Sun itself, lauded for its "light" and its "full heat" (35:20–21; poem 39), is linked often to Allah, the "Lord" or "Cleaver" of the "Daybreak" (6:97; poem 12; 113:1; poems 74, 134); thus it is supremely fitting "at the dawning of each day" to "seek forgiveness" (51:18; poem 50). But for Rumi, fire is nothing less than triumphant joy amid life's afflictions, and so he not only affirms it but blends it with his second major metaphor, that of the dance. For Rumi, when Mt. Sinai trembled at the granting of the decalogue it really danced; so too, when the fires were cooled for Abraham, he danced — in flame (7:143; poem 85) as, on a far lower level of being which yet has emblematic power, the very atoms or particles of dust dance daily in the sun (51:56; poem 104). Our souls, like Abraham and like the legendary salamander, are by nature adapted to the light as to the heat (21:51–69; poem 95). Fire and dance, for Rumi, are the same in essence: glad affirmation, rejoicing, amid trial.

The poet puns on *bala* ("yes") and *balā* ("affliction") to make the point that suffering is one with affirmation; the very trees and rivers danced at the primordial moment when they confessed their Maker (7:172; poem 86). There is a lifegiving interchange: we owe everything to Allah, but as we are His instruments, He needs us to do His arduous work (8:17; poem 87). Our lives are a response to Allah's gift, our acceptance of His blessing of *amāna* or trust (33:72; poem 91). Muhammad's steed Buraq may be allegorized as the Love of Allah, Who has trusted His servants (17:1; poem 92). Our higher soul is the Jesus that, like Mary, we bear in pain and travail (19:23–26; poem 93). Rumi's own greatest sorrow was the death of his spiritual comrade, Shams-i Tabrīz, whose first name means "Sun." Yet after the death of Shams, Rumi saw the friend's fiery spirit alive in solar light, in morning star, in burning bush.

A voice of peace and healing love, Rumi reframes the Qur'anic emphasis on the redeemability of humanity from its drive to bloodshed through its capacity to be dyed clean in the vat of Allah (2:30, 138; poem 77). Confronted with a Qur'anic verse that speaks of those who "fight in the way of Allah and shall slay and be slain," Rumi interprets the struggle as simply the combat of spring with winter when the lilies sharpen the "swords and daggers" of their emergent leaves (9:111–112; poem 88). We may see the lily as Moses' wondrous white hand (20:22; 28–32; poem 94). A patient Jacob, spring lay dormant before being awakened as by Joseph's prophecy-enabling shirt (12:91–96; poem 89). Allah's mercy is a freshening rain (21:107; poem 96). Captivating and endearing is the symbolic moment when, after the death of Shams, Rumi marks the chiming sounds of hammers in a goldsmiths' bazaar and whirls up his new friend Salahuddin Zarkub in a spontaneous dervish-dance of triumphant ecstasy, a universal, deeply personal joy (poem 121). Here, as in his many books about Shams as Allah-mirroring Sun, Rumi becomes one of the world's great celebrators of the soul falling in love. His love lyrics can be not only mystical but often wonderfully funny (poem 123); like Shakespeare, he encompasses much.

A soarer into mystic heights, Rumi likens himself to the clay bird given life by Jesus' breath (5:110; poem 80). Rumi has an invulnerably sanguine temperament; he likes to contrast the optimism of the smiling Jesus to the pessimism of a distrustful John the Baptist (poem 117). There is such a serene equanimity and unshakable gladness to Rumi's thought that even within the emptiness of the Void, the non-being or *'adam* from which the universe arose, the death from which life originally came, Rumi can find a potential for creativity, somewhat in the manner, I would suggest, of Hegel's philosophic Nothingness or *Nichts* (6:96; poem 82), a surprisingly active, generative power. For Rumi, the average human soul is like the camel, in the parable told by Jesus and Muhammad, which cannot enter the metaphoric needle's eye: at night the soul-camel enters the darkness of divine non-being but is blind to the splendor of that void's inexhaustible potency as matrix of life (7:40–42; poem 84).

Yet there is a tendency in Rumi, at times, toward an other-worldliness that can make strikingly pejorative allegoric use of the creatures of our earthly world. The spider becomes for him the selfish person who takes impious pride in his own art (29:41; poem 100). The donkey's ugly bray soon turns the beast, for Rumi, into an emblem of the crudity of our sensory world (31:19; 62:5; poem 102). He likes to contrast the transcendent rising of Muhammad's Buraq to the heavy, unrescued earthiness of a donkey. The juxtaposition can open up entertaining satiric possibilities. But, becoming a bit impatient, after a while, with Rumi's lofty strictures, it occurred to me that I might stage a helpful debate between the sometimes abstracted, upward-gazing Rumi and the wise but earthier Nasreddin Hodja, Turkey's beloved thirteenth-century comic hero, a contemporary of Rumi, who also spent much of his later life in Turkey. In poem 102 you can hear this fictional debate, presented in a seriocomic parable of my devising (see also poem 122).

Finally, I turn briefly to the seven East-informed Western mentors to whom I am most deeply indebted for making my East-West project possible: J. W. von Goethe, Adam Mickiewicz, Alexander Pushkin, Mohammed Marmaduke Pickthall, Annemarie Schimmel, Karen Armstrong, and Katharina Mommsen. I begin with Goethe, whose poetry book called *West-East Divan* (1819; a "divan" is an assemblage, a collection) represents a momentous cultural breakthrough not adequately appreciated even now. The book's deeply researched, pioneering poems range widely over topics from Zoroastrian fire veneration to the role of houris in Islamic heaven; it is impossible to summarize here the treasures the volume contains. But I can say a few words about the great poet's Qur'anic responses, which have been decisively influential on my other mentors and on me.

Even as the Qur'anic assurance "[t]hat ye shall journey on from plane to plane" (84:19; poem 61) seems echoed in Goethe's ideal of ascent "to new spheres of pure activity" (*Faust* l. 705), so the German cultural mediator wrote in his *West-East Divan* a quatrain-motto developing the Qur'anic theme of Allah as "Lord of the East and the West" (73:9; poem 59; 2:142; poems 78, 79):

> To God belongs the Orient,
> To God belongs the Occident;
> The Northern and the Southern lands
> Resting, tranquil, in His hands.

In a related lyric not included in the *Divan* collection he adds:

> Who knows himself and others well
> No longer may ignore:
> Orient, Occident can dwell
> Separately no more.

Goethe often seeks for Allah's guidance, echoing the Qur'anic "Seven Most Recited," the initial brief sura which is in part a prayer that one may be directed to the "straight path" when led "astray" (1:5–7; poem 76). He likes to vary the Qur'anic theme of the stars that emblemize Allah's guidance (6:98; poem 81). And he adds in the *Divan*:

> I find it folly, and quite odd,
> That stubborn folk seek to deny:
> If "Islam" means we all serve God,
> We all in Islam live and die.

At the same time, Goethe can see the wit and humor in the Qur'an. I have noted the comic awkwardness of the flustered friends of Potiphar's wife in the Qur'anic retelling of the Joseph tale. Goethe finds a kind of playfulness even in a satiric remark by Allah (22:15; poem 97). The German poet himself writes a playful reply to a Rumi quatrain in a witty four-liner of Zuleika (28:88; poem 99). There is a wonderful lightness, as well, to Goethe's lyric, "Favored Animals," where he rethinks the Islamic theme of scriptural animals deemed worthy of heavenly reward (poem 114). Goethe jokes about donkeys, even the one that Jesus rode, in a tradition going back to some allegorizing by Rumi (poems 118, 119). I even detect a subtle, though more serious, wit in Goethe's versifying of a highly valuable "fetwa" of Ebusu'ud (poem 127). Emboldened by Goethe, I try a bit of humor myself in poem 126, where my stubborn typographical errors are imaged as the work of intractable jinns.

Further, in a Goethean spirit of lively colloquy with my mentors East and West, I actually carry on a number of dialogues with Rumi in which I propose alternative metaphors to those he employed. When Rumi portrays the human soul as the Lord's faithful falcon, I suggest, in reply, another model: the eagle that, rising, is wondrously empowered to look at the sun (89:23–28; poem 106). When Rumi tells an allegoric tale of love as a mirror, I counter this, in lyrical conversation, by positing the alternative image of a rival inner dawn (poem 120). My *East-West Poetry*, like the Goethean *West-East Divan* whose title it echoes in homage, is a book of dialogues. In the noble game of rival metaphors, no single insight has to "win."

Before reluctantly leaving Goethe, I want to suggest how not only his *Divan* but also the immensely informative *Notes and Essays* he appended to it nourish the comparative imaginings of today's reader. It was noted above that the reverent Qur'anic portrayal of the child Jesus as already a mature teacher, and of the youthful Jesus as Allah-aided miracle-worker lending life to a clay bird, would stimulate Persian poets to write their own parables about Jesus. Here I translate one such parable from the German rendition that Goethe offers in the "General Observations" part of the *Notes and Essays*; it is a small masterpiece by twelfth-century poet Nizami:

> As Jesus wandered through the world
> He passed, one day, a marketplace.
> Along the path, a dead dog lay,
> Dragged to a nearby house's door.
> A group stood by the carrion
> As vultures round cadavers crowd.
> And one said: "That offensive smell
> Will utterly wipe out my brain."
> And one: "It's more than I can take.
> What graves reject brings dreadful luck."
> So each one sang, to his own tune,
> The dead dog's body to disdain.
> But now, when it was Jesus' turn,
> He spoke, without reviling, kind.
> In his warmhearted way, he said:
> "The teeth are white as any pearls."
> Hearing the words, the people felt,
> Like glowing mussels, burning hot.

I have read collections of new Jesus tales authored by writers of the last few centuries, but, unaware of Persian legacies, the Western compilers regrettably included no Islamic contributions.

Adam Mickiewicz and Alexander Pushkin, respectively the most highly esteemed poets of Poland and Russia, are intercultural mediators in the Goethean *Divan* tradition who helped activate the imagination at work in my East-West poems. *Crimean Sonnets* (1826), the Polish singer's finest lyrics in this form, made me want to write East-West replies, as the Qur'an itself would do later. I can offer here, in my translation, only a brief sample of Mickiewicz's work and outlook, Sonnet 6, "Bakhtchisaray at Night":

> Leaving the mosque, the pious move in each direction.
> The muezzin's call is muffled in the evening peace;
> Faded the twilight's ruby face, the light's release.
> Silver King Night his dear one seeks, warm predilection.
>
> They shine in heaven's harem, stars in timeless order.
> Moving among them, on a sapphire wave, is gliding
> A cloud, upon a seeming dreamtide, swanlike, riding,
> With breast of white, edged by a thin, gold-tinted border.

From cypresses and minarets — the shade of night.
Beyond are circled forms, giants of granite black
As demons that might sit in Eblis' council room

In a dark tent and, sometimes, shining at the height
A lightning bolt awakes — horseman Farís come back —
Flies through the silent wildness, heaven's empty gloom.

(See my *A Poetic Dialogue with Adam Mickiewicz: The "Crimean Sonnets" Trans-lated, with Sonnet Preface, Sonnet Replies, and Notes* [Bernstein-Verlag 2007], 66.) Mickiewicz, in his Crimean exile, transformed himself into one of the major lyricists of the Romantic age, blending his deepest feelings with the heritage of Middle Eastern and Islamic lore, much as Goethe had done.

Another East-West traveler in the Goethean tradition is Alexander Pushkin, whose nine "Imitations of the Koran" (1826), the direct progenitors of my lyrical responses here, are as powerful as they are varied in topic and treat-ment. But rather than quote from this cycle, I would rather offer an ex-traordinary short poem I translated some years ago. Pushkin's "Prophet" is not only the poet's finest lyric but his culminating East-West achievement. If you will first read poem 67 in this book, you will immediately recognize the provenance of Pushkin's lyric tale in the hadith account of the heart-cleansing of Muhammad! The parallel seems never to have been noticed by Pushkin critics. Here, then, is Pushkin's "Prophet":

Tormented by a thirst of spirit,
I cursed the barren earth that bore me.
Crawling, I reached a crossroads. Near it
A six-winged seraph flamed before me.
He touched, with fingers dreamy-light,
The pupils of my eyes. Affright
Opened my wizard pupils wide,
Like to an eagle terrified.
He touched my ears, which then were filled
With rushing, roaring clangor. Thrilled,
I felt the trembling of the sky,
The flight of angels overhead,
The sea beasts' underwater tread,
The valley vineyards' growth. While I
Lay there, he touched my trembling mouth
And tore my sinful tongue out. Drouth
Was all it had deserved, so sly

And idle. The wise serpent's sting
He, with his right hand bloodying
My lips benumbed beyond a sigh,
Inserted. With his sword my breast
He clove, took out the trembling heart,
Then put in, at the Lord's behest,
An ardent flaming coal. Apart
From all things living as I lay,
I heard God's voice within me say,
Prophet, arise! Behold! And hearken!
Make your spirit one with me.
Cross lands that lighten, seas that darken,
And with the flame word, set hearts free.

(See *The Paterson Literary Review* 32 (2003) ed. Maria Mazziotti Gillan, 217.) Dostoevsky liked to recite this poem aloud, and he repeatedly did so in public with electrifying drama.

My East-West collection would be inconceivable without *The Meaning of the Glorious Koran: An Explanatory Translation* by [Mohammed] Marmaduke Pickthall (Knopf 1930; repr. Everyman 1992). I have consulted several Qur'ans, with diverse merits: notably A. J. Arberry, *The Koran Interpreted: A Translation* (2 vols. London 1955; repr. Oxford 1999), attentive to the precise wording of the Arabic; and A. Yusuf Ali, *The Holy Qur'an: Text, Translation and Commentary* (McGregor and Werner 1946), invaluable for thousands of notes and an ample index. But only Pickthall conveyed to me the musical joy that would generate hymns (poem 111 is my song of homage). Often his phrases would turn, at the slightest urging, into refrains that summoned forth in me strophes which, while writing them, I imagined sung or chanted by a soloist and choir. His phrases were canorous, encouraging me to "sing" long lines in the sweeping rhythms he had come upon, or brief ones to echo the pithiness of his compact melodic phrases. I chose Pickthall's Qur'an because it had chosen me (poem 112).

The Qur'an when read aloud, in musically chanted Arabic, is said to be a transforming experience for the hearer. Armstrong writes that "the most frequent cause of conversion" to Islam in the early years of the faith "was the Qur'an itself," whose "extreme beauty" evidently "penetrated people's reserves" (125). For "it seems that the extraordinary beauty of the recited Arabic touched something deeply buried and resonated with the unconscious longings and aspirations of those who heard it" (101). On a lesser level, my own lyrical responses need to be read aloud, or heard declaimed by an inner voice. Every day, for months, I would read Pickthall and then begin to hear sonnets or hymns or many-strophe'd songs rise out of his Qur'an phrases. Always strong-rhythmed, they usually rhymed as well for a more intricate and moving music. On occasion (poems 14, 23, 33, 39, 50) Pickthall's Qur'anic utterance would have a musical shape that engendered a stanza form freshly invented. All my poems are metered. You can use the indentations as guides to the number of feet per line: metric feet are structure units, usually two-syllable groups called iambs (weak STRONG) or trochees (STRONG weak), singable rhythms.

Annemarie Schimmel is affectionately renamed "Annemarumi" in my lyric of homage (poem 124), and it is to her that I owe my rich experience of Rumi's poetic thought, symbols, and lifeworld. This polymathic scholar has helped in every stage and aspect of my growing understanding of Islam-related cultural tradition: poem 113, for instance, describes the double rose Schimmel explains as bearing the ninety-nine names of God and of His Prophet, respectively written on two blossoms branching from one stem. Now, even though my *East-West Poetry* is complete, I am still as likely to pick a chapter from one of many books by "Annemarumi" (listed in "Acknowledgments" and given in many poem epigraphs where I quote her) as to choose a sura of Pickthall's Qur'an when I seek writing inspiration through bibliomancy, or the interpretation of spirit-arousing passages found by chance. The other day I picked up Schimmel's excellent volume *The Mystery of Numbers* (Oxford 1993), where I learned that the Arabic words for tulip, moon, and Allah each have a numerological value totaling sixty-six (using the alphabet-letters as numbers). I responded to this in "Personal Numerology," a grateful tribute to her:

> *Laláh, hilál, Alláh,* the tulip, moon, and Lord,
> Combine for me in you, my six and sixtieth year:
> Innumerable do the lunar curves appear
> Upon the plate where, triple-pronged, like blood
>   outpoured,
>
> The tulip, calyx blue, green leaved, a hidden hoard
> Of symbols in the number cited we revere
> Brings in a threefold leap of rooted bloom, a clear
> And clarion Allah-call that ev'n the jinns adored.
>
> The number of a light, flow'r, God my life attains
> To say with numerals what glad Aladdin gains:
> For see the double *waw,* twins facing, that explains

The outward bending swell of magic lamp: it seems
The form of arms enfolded, sultan seen in dreams.
Ready to rub, the six-and-six in genie gleams.

Karen Armstrong has mentored me philosophically through her exemplary *A History of God* (Random 1993), where I learned that in the Middle Ages and for a good while thereafter, Islamic philosophy was fully as rich, diverse, ingenious, and penetrating as the Christian and Jewish varieties. Then, in *Muhammad: A Biography of the Prophet* (Phoenix 2001), she gave me a lively sense of what the Prophet must have been like as a living human being confronting an extraordinary mission and a more than difficult situation. A sonnet of mine in response to her narrative was offered earlier.

Finally, I acknowledge Katharina Mommsen (poem 133) not only as chief mentor of my East-West verse writing and Qur'an interpretation project, but as my esteemed colleague, counselor, encourager, and friend. Her many East-West books and essays, focusing notably on Goethe's pioneering interpretations of the Middle East in the *West-East Divan* and elsewhere, though translated into many languages, are not yet available in English, but I am gladdened by the fact that her *Goethe und der Islam* is currently being rendered by Lane Jennings. In poem 108 I make reference to an event that has had crucial consequences — for Goethe, for Prof. Mommsen, and most lately for me. In the fall of 1813 Goethe acquired a page of the Qur'an in Persian and Arabic, containing the concluding brief chapter, sura 114, an appeal to seek refuge in God (poem 75). A soldier arriving in Goethe's hometown had brought the page with him from Spain during the Napoleonic Wars. The German poet copied the adorned sura gift in Arabic, and he tried to learn as much as he could about it. The results of that decades-long search have enriched us all. I have continued that quest, in spirit, here.

Goethe's precedent-setting *Divan* founded a tradition of intercultural verse-dialogue that I seek to continue. So my book is East-West in outlook from first page to last. In poem 1, I cite Percy Bysshe Shelley's *Adonais* lii.462–3 to suggest how the Qur'an reveals the One in the many. In poem 48 I pay tribute to fourteenth-century storyteller Giovanni Boccaccio ("the fabler") and eighteenth-century philosopher-dramatist Gotthold Ephraim Lessing ("the playwright") for their profoundly conceived, shared metaphor (found respectively in the *Decameron* and *Nathan the Wise*) of the three great Abrahamic religions as "three rings" of high value. In poem 132 I liken the teaching of Buddha, as expounded by Western thinker Pema Chödrön (now known by her Buddhist name), to that of Allah for their effectiveness in cleansing the spirit and removing rancor from the heart. In poem 138 I acknowledge St. Francis, St. John of the Cross (San Juan de la Cruz), and Angelus Silesius (pen name of Johannes Scheffler) as co-contributors to the wealth of worldwide mystic writing along with Islamic sages Baba Tahir, Hallaj, Yunus, and Rumi. And in poems 139 and 140, I end the book with a reverie of the vastly influential philosopher Hegel, who loved Hafiz and Rumi, as offering to us the emblem of a Hafizian candle, then himself becoming a Rumi-like Sufi dervish dancer. A bit whimsical, perhaps, my departing East-West reverie is both as serious and as light-hearted as Mevlana — again, I hope, in a Goethean spirit of imaginative mobility and eagerness to learn.

Acknowledgments and Sources

My *East-West Poetry* would never have come into being without the invaluable stimulus and continual heartfelt encouragement of my friend and distinguished colleague Katharina Mommsen, who for over half a century in a series of brilliant works has pioneered the study of Goethe's epoch-making encounter with the cultures of the Middle East. She has corresponded with me regularly, and her willingness to read my lyrical responses to Islamic tradition as soon as I produced them has been tremendously helpful. Her deep insight into Goethe, Islam, the Qur'an, and the Middle East has influenced a number of the poems offered here. I will never be able to express my gratitude to her. She introduced me also to the work of the late Annemarie Schimmel, whose extraordinarily illuminating books I quote in many of the poems' epigraphs: without the treasury of ideas and images provided by this incomparable student of Islamic cultures, neither the second nor the third part of the present work could have been imagined. The scriptural rendering I use throughout is [Mohammed] Marmaduke Pickthall's *The Meaning of the Glorious Koran: An Explanatory Translation* (Knopf 1930, rpt., Random House/Everyman's Library 1992). It is the most musically evocative, literarily effective, and visually vivid rendition I have found in English, and it made me feel with startling power the profound poetry of the Qur'an. The works by Schimmel cited in epigraphs are *And Muhammad Is His Messenger: The Veneration of the Prophet in Islamic Piety* (Chapel Hill: Univ. of North Carolina Press, 1985); *As Through a Veil: Mystical Poetry of Islam* (Oxford: Oneworld, 2001); *Islam: An Introduction* (Albany: SUNY Press, 1992); *Mystical Dimensions of Islam* (Chapel Hill: Univ. of North Carolina Press, 1975); *Rumi's World: The Life and Work of the Great Sufi Poet* (Boston: Shambhala, 2001); *The Triumphal Sun: A Study of the Works of Jalāloddin Rumi* (Albany, SUNY Press, 1993). All Goethe translations are my own. I owe gratitude to Dr. Petra Hardt of Insel Verlag for permission to translate Rilke's "Mohammeds Berufung." I want to thank Beverly Comstock for her indispensable computer expertise and aid, and Lori Vandermark-Fuller, Jennifer Winans, and Matthew Tynan for their devoted assistance in helping me prepare the manuscript for publication.

PART 1

Lyrical Responses to the Qur'an

1.

Lyrical Response to Sura 1
"The Opening"

In the name of Allah, the Beneficent, the Merciful.

1. Praise be to Allah, Lord of the Worlds,

2. The Beneficent, the Merciful.

3. Owner of the Day of Judgment,

4. Thee (alone) we worship; Thee (alone) we ask for help.

5. Show us the straight path,

6. The path of those whom Thou hast favoured;

7. Not (the path) of those who earn Thine anger nor of those who go astray.

"Time, like a dome of many-colored glass,
Stains the white radiance of eternity."
So poet Shelley wrote. In things that pass,
The many that are born and die, is He,

So we may say, reflected. Such are we.
One was Creation; seven were the days.
"The Seven of the Oft-Repeated" praise
The One they mirror everlastingly.

Varying, patterned cantillation may,
When faithful to the spirit of the One,
Multiply coloring, the benison

Widen by tributaries of our hearts,
Combining in their amiable arts,
As rivers to the Ocean lead the way.

2.

Lyrical Response to Verses from Sura 2
"The Cow" and Sura 33 "The Clans"

2:31. And He taught Adam all the names, then showed them to the angels, saying: Inform me of the names of these, if ye are truthful.

32. They said: Be glorified! We have no knowledge saving that which Thou hast taught us. Lo! thou, only thou, art the Knower, the Wise.

33. He said: O Adam! Inform them of their names, and when he had informed them of their names, He said: Did I not tell you that I know the secret of the heavens and the earth? . . . .

. . . . .

33.56. Lo! Allah and His angels shower blessings on the Prophet.

And He taught Adam all the names, then showed them to the angels,
Saying, Inform me of the names of these, if ye are truthful.
They said, We have no knowledge saving that which Thou hast taught us.
So Adam taught them truthful names, the earth's and heaven's secrets.

Lo! Allah and His angels shower blessings on the Prophet.
Were Adam also worthy of that raptured benediction?
Some commentators claim that he knew all the names of Allah...
Yet any name at all is testament to a creating.

A namer — prophet, poet, mage — is bearer of a message.
A noun before unknown reveals an undiscovered creature.
A verb yet unconceived brings forth an action in the planning.
New adjective an attribute will add to senses' pleasure.

A novel adverb amplifies a move or state of being.
New-made conjunctions fortify the logic of cognition.
Unheard of interjections are the heraldry of feeling.
Even an added article may place a thing more clearly.

What of a rearrangement of the layout of a language?
That will be nothing less than redesigning our conception.
A structure of imagining needs names to be engendered
And cannot be a gift bequeathed without more change of naming.

A "locovore," who thrives on local food, embodies knowledge.
Take a "staycation"; you may see the brightness all about you.
Savor "endotic" stimuli, delight in what is nearest.
Or try all three: your philosophic wisdom will be tripled.

3.

Lyrical Response to Verses from Sura 2 "The Cow"

---

31. And He taught Adam all the names, then showed them to the angels, saying: Inform me of the names of these, if ye are truthful.

32. They said: Be glorified! We have no knowledge saving that which Thou hast taught us. Lo! Thou, only Thou, art the Knower, the Wise.

33. He said: O Adam! Inform them of their names, and when he had informed them of their names, He said: Did I not tell you that I know the secret of the heavens and the earth? And I know that which ye disclose and which ye hide.

34. And when We said unto the Angels: Prostrate yourselves before Adam, they fell prostrate, all save Iblis [Satan]. He demurred through pride, and so became a disbeliever.

Re-tell the story of the colored coat
Of Joseph and the high prophetic dreams
With even brighter myriad rainbow-gleams;
Then mark the brothers' envy, and take note:

The singling out of one with sunlike, wise,
And heaven-blent discernment — Adam here —
Awakes temptation, danger. We may fear
The aftermath. Would Adam realize,

Like Joseph, holy generosity
Could warmly set the soul from rancor free,
Scattering the remains of jealousy?

Or will he, knowing, naming cleverly —
Forgetting Higher Pow'r, however — fly,
In Iblis-mood, too far in pride, and die?

4.

Lyrical Response to a Verse from Sura 2 "The Cow"

177. It is not righteousness that ye turn your faces to the East and the West; but righteous is he who believeth in Allah and the Last Day and the angels and the Scripture and the Prophets; and giveth his wealth, for love of Him, to kinsfolk and to orphans and the needy and the wayfarer and to those who ask, and to set slaves free; and observeth proper worship and payeth the poor-due. And Those who keep their treaty when they make one, and the patient in tribulation and adversity and time of stress. Such are they who are sincere. Such are the God-fearing.

"Tribula" is a threshing-sledge, and tribulation
Properly borne may help a harvest come to be.
It is no virtue merest ritual to see
As adequate for happy spirit-habitation.

Wisely interpreted, each turning lends belief.
East, and the sun of Allah-prophecy will rise.
West, find the sober carmine light, to mind the skies
Kindly of harvest color and the reaper-sheaf.

South, and the noontide bounty overspreads the land.
North, and the challenge boreal revives the will.
For love of Him who oversees the well and ill,

The fed and hungry, turn, wherever you may stand,
About in each direction, seeking whom to aid.
Of messengers of brother-love are angels made.

5.

Lyrical Response to Verses from Sura 2 "The Cow"

---

256. There is no compulsion in religion. The right direction is henceforth distinct from error. And he who rejecteth false deities and believeth in Allah has grasped a firm handhold which will never break. Allah is Hearer, Knower.

. . . . .

261. The likeness of those who spend their wealth in Allah's way is as the likeness of a grain which groweth seven ears; in every ear a hundred grains. Allah giveth increase manifold to whom He will. Allah is All-Embracing, All-Knowing.

There's no compulsion in religion. Though the right
Way may be known to all, you get to walk what road
You will. The yoke is easy, shouldering the load
Upon the path well chosen, yet no higher might

Can make you take it. Liberty within is light.
The Sun of Heaven to the lower eye has owed
The joy of choice. The inner godly ray may goad,
But spirit and desire are one in double might.

Wise aims of action may be known by their results.
What's fruitful will reward, and so the soul exults.
Sowing good seed in widest throw-curve catapults,

Proportioned to the goal, the widespread wealth afar.
You cannot know how great the implications are.
The sun, a godly eye, guides growth, a glowing star.

6.

Lyrical Response to a Verse from Sura 3
"The Family of 'Imrân"

---

37. And her Lord accepted her with full acceptance and vouchsafed to her a goodly growth and made Zachariah her guardian. Whenever Zachariah went into the sanctuary where she was, he found that she had food. He said: O Mary! Whence cometh unto thee this (food)? She answered: It is from Allah. Allah giveth without stint to whom He will.

Whenever Zachariah carefully would enter
The sanctuary where young Virgin Mary was,
He found her well supplied with holy food because
Of grace the ministrations of high Allah lent her.

The sanctuary or enclosure is the room
To which the word *mahríb* is in the text assigned.
Today it means a niche with Meccan rays aligned
For praying, and the verse the alcove may illume.

By mahríb-sheltered modest meditative thought
Nourishment to the Virgin daily had been brought.
So, too, for worshipers are fruitful bounties wrought.

Like Mary is the Muslim, praying near the text
That hints of chosenness in this world and the next,
And of the oneness of the seeker and the Sought.

7.

Lyrical Response to Verses from Sura 3 "The Family of 'Imrân" and Sura 42 "Counsel"

3:133. And vie with one another for forgiveness from your Lord, and for a Paradise as wide as are the heavens and the earth, prepared for those who ward off (evil);

134. Those who spend (of that which Allah hath given them) in ease and in adversity, those who control their wrath and are forgiving toward mankind; Allah loveth the good;

135. And those who, when they do an evil thing or wrong themselves, remember Allah and implore forgiveness for their sins — Who forgiveth sins save Allah only? — and will not knowingly repeat (the wrong) they did.

136. The reward of such will be forgiveness from their Lord, and Gardens underneath which rivers flow, wherein they will abide for ever — a bountiful reward for workers!

42:43. And verily whoso is patient and forgiveth — lo! that, verily, is (of) the steadfast heart of things.

And vie with one another for forgiveness from your Lord;
And for a Paradise as wide as heavens and the earth;
And spend, in ease and in adversity, what Allah gives;
And be forgiving to mankind, for Allah loves the good.

And those who, when they do an evil thing or wrong themselves
(These are the same), recall their wiser mind, controlling wrath,
Remember Allah, and implore forgiveness for their sins
And will not knowingly repeat the wrong that they have done,

Lo! the reward of such will be forgiveness from their God
(For who forgiveth sin save Allah only?); they shall have
Gardens whereunder rivers flow, and there will they abide
Forever with a tranquil heart for pardon and for love.

Now lend an ear to hear the river coursing through a song
Made of the words of Allah from the East unto the West,
Seven the heartbeats (number of Creation) in the strain
Of thankfulness for love dispensed in bounty to the wise.

The hands that clap, the feet that dance, replying to the sky,
The voice to echo bounding water, breakers of the sea,
The quiet word within the mind, bestirred at sunset hour,
The rising choir moved upward by the flame beyond the wave,

The patience and the pardon at the steadfast heart of things
Which are the higher mercy of a soul that knows to hark
And heed, to wait and hear, to hope and reach, to breathe in peace
Will aid us daily in our measured calm of sounding praise.

8.

Lyrical Response to Verses from Sura 4 "Women"

---

9. And let those fear (in their behaviour toward orphans) who if they left behind them weak offspring would be afraid for them. So let them mind their duty to Allah, and speak justly.

10. Lo! those who devour the wealth of orphans wrongfully, they do but swallow fire into their bellies, and they will be exposed to burning flame.

'Tis a similitude, this belly-flaming hell.
For thieves of orphans' wealth a simile would tell
Of wretchedness. Yet elements aren't one but four.
Of heaven and of hell they offer metaphor.

Reavers of orphans are deprived of vital air;
A conscience-rock intolerable they will bear.
From them the life-providing river shrinks away.
Quaternally deserted, self-tormented they.

Creative energy is fire unto the wise.
Deep breathing is our Being, singing to the skies.
Partly of water is our flowing blood, our birth.
Made taller by the trees, we walk on solid earth.

The moral mind transforms the elemental scheme:
Infernal or ethereal? — our worldly theme.

9.

Lyrical Response to Verses from Sura 5 "The Table Spread"

---

27. But recite unto them with a truth the tale of the two sons of Adam, how they offered each a sacrifice, and it was accepted from the one of them and it was not accepted from the other. (The one) said: I will surely kill thee. (The other) answered: Allah accepteth only from those who ward off (evil).

28. Even if thou stretch out thy hand against me to kill me, I shall not stretch out my hand against thee to kill thee, lo! I fear Allah, the Lord of the Worlds.
. . . . .

32. For that cause We decreed for the Children of Israel that whosoever killeth a human being for other than manslaughter or corruption in the earth, it shall be as if he had killed all mankind, and who saveth the life of one, it shall be as if had saved the life of all mankind.

How can it be? To save the life of one
Is like the rescuing of humankind?
Qualities are immeasurable things.
To kill a brother — infinitely sad

Although a finite creature-life is done.
Boundless the worth of each, to those not blind.
One man, in cold objective reckonings,
Only one more than nothing? That is mad!

For he is infinitely more. The sun
With titan eye again will never find
An Abel. So the living scripture sings:
Each Adam-child, made God-alike, is glad.

One saving is unending benison.
Who kills but one — to untold woe consigned.
Deeds ill, or good, are vast engenderings —
Of darkness, or of heart-life heaven-clad.

10.

Lyrical Response to Verses from Sura 5
"The Table Spread"

---

44. Lo! We did reveal the Torah, wherein is guidance and a light. . . .

46. And we caused Jesus, son of Mary, to follow in their footsteps. . . . We bestowed on him the Gospel wherein is guidance and a light. . . .

There are tables fully spread whereon the measure of delight
Is more grandly, amply granted than the seeker yet may see.
Narrow gaze prevents partaking of that banquet readily.
Lo! We did reveal the Torah, where is guidance and a light.

Unexpected the expanse, and wide-encompassing the sight
As in mind we ramble, travel on the soil or sand or scree
In the storm or calm; by sun or moon; warm, cool; wild, footloose, free.
We bestowed on him the Gospel where is guidance and a light.

David, Solomon could learn of birds and animals aright
From a summer psalming, springtime singing, fall exalting. We
Of a starry dust are made, as they — same electricity.
Lo! We did reveal the Torah, where is guidance and a light.

Everlasting is the life-drive from the depth and to the height,
Fire in sky and sunken, drunken-whirling endless energy.
Proton, neutron, and electron — spurring-spinning trinity.
We bestowed on him the Gospel, where is guidance and a light.

For the mind can bird the trees and shark the seas and star the night,
Germ the wheat, and colden flurry-snow, in cosmic body be
A theurgic world, emboldened by a vim-divinity:
Lo! We did reveal the Torah, where is guidance and a light.

It is only in a choir that we the love of life requite.
Harm we bravely may sublate within a human harmony.
Let the body model mind: we find we frame a symmetry.
We bestowed on him the Gospel where is guidance and a light.

As the one hand aids the other, so the wise combine their might
In the loving touch of oneness, and the blood that speedily
To the brain will rise in brightness fills with Life the Eden-tree.
Torah, Gospel, Islam, lyre-hymn be a guidance and a light.

11.

Lyrical Response to a Verse from Sura 5
"The Table Spread"

---

110. . . . . Allah saith: O Jesus, son of Mary! Remember my favour unto thee and unto thy mother; how I strengthened thee with the holy Spirit, so that thou spakest unto mankind in the cradle as in maturity; and how I taught thee the Scripture and Wisdom and Torah and the Gospel; and how thou didst shape of clay as it were the likeness of a bird by My permission, and didst blow upon it and it was a bird by My permission. . . .

Allah taught Jesus how the holy Spirit swept
Breathlike over the water (as from Noah's ark
A later dove would leave and sweep above the dark)
Impregnating the depths that yet in dream-life slept.

'Twould be this very Wind of Light that lively leapt
Into the lungs of Adam, earth of Adamah,
The while the angels cried and hymned their high hurrah.
O breath of life, that hope awake in us have kept!

Allah permitted Jesus now to replicate
With bird of earth a miracle unheard of. Great
The grace upon the image of the God bestowed.

This re-enactor of the birth of man bestrode,
Grateful, the ground whereof the bird and man were made.
We are but potter's clay without Creator's aid.

12.

Lyrical Response to Verses from Sura 6 "Cattle"

96. Lo! Allah (it is) who splitteth the grain of corn and the date-stone (for sprouting). He bringeth forth the living from the dead, and is the bringer-forth of the dead from the living. . . .

97. He is the Cleaver of the Daybreak, and He hath appointed the night for stillness, and the sun and the moon for reckoning. That is the measuring of the Mighty, the Wise. . . .

100. He it is Who sendeth down water from the sky, and therewith We bring forth buds of every kind; We bring forth the green blade from which we bring forth the thick-clustered grain; and from the date-palm, from the pollen thereof, spring pendant bunches; and (We bring forth) gardens of grapes, and the olive and the pomegranate, alike and unlike. Look upon the fruit thereof, when they bear fruit, and upon its ripening. . . .

The grain of corn, the date-stone, split for sprouting — these
Vary the death-to-life and rest-to-waking theme
That is our nightly-daily in-out breathing scheme;
The dark for stillness and the morning harmonies

Joined by the Cleaver of the Daybreak. As in dream,
Thick-clustered wheat and heavy-pendant bunches of
Palm-dates from pollen, pomegranate, olive — love
Is here, and in the trees that with sweet fruitage teem!

From the descending water, bud and blade arise
Attesting the prolific wedding of the skies
And earth that in the Song of Solomon we heard

Exalted. He and Sheba saw the bodied word
In radiant nature for their passion that would pass
From wind and storm to reeds and branching trees and grass.

13.

Lyrical Response to a Verse from Sura 6 "Cattle"

---

126. And whomsoever it is Allah's will to guide, He expandeth his bosom unto the Surrender, and whomsoever it is His will to send astray, He maketh his bosom close and narrow as if he were engaged in sheer ascent....

Expand your bosom unto the Surrender who
From fetters have not freed the soul in prison pent
By stern demand of narrow self-concern, that you
May not be stifled, pale, engaged in sheer ascent.

Expand your bosom unto the Surrender, for
The one to whom an Allah-rooted pow'r is lent
As by an angel, makes the hour an open door,
Is never stifled, pale, engaged in sheer ascent.

Expand your bosom unto the Surrender. We
For whom the music of the mentor-flute is meant
Can feel as one in sweet symmetric melody
And not be stifled, pale, engaged in sheer ascent.

Expand your bosom unto the Surrender. Eye
Of Allah, seen upon the morn of orient,
Lends life to them that are begotten, born, and die.
They'll not be stifled, pale, engaged in sheer ascent.

Expand your bosom unto the Surrender. When
Embraving for a task, inhale with strong intent
Although in stress, the exhalation sweeter then,
Not to be stifled, pale, engaged in sheer ascent.

Expand your bosom unto the Surrender. Will
That every breath may be an energy well spent,
In give-and-take of air shared pleasure to fulfil,
And never stifled, pale, engaged in sheer ascent.

Expand your bosom unto the Surrender — so
Not giving up, or giving out. The breath you're sent —
Let it be treasured. Let it be. And let it go.
And never stifled, pale, engaged in sheer ascent.

14.

Lyrical Response to Verses from Sura 6
"Cattle"

136. Say (O Muhammad): O my people! Work according to your power. Lo! I too am working. Thus ye will come to know for which of us will be the happy sequel. . . .

165. . . . Each soul earneth only on its own account, nor doth any laden bear another's load. . . .

Say (O Muhammad): O my people! work
According to your power. Lo! I too
Am working. Thereby ye will come to know
For which of us will be the happy sequel.

Fell lethargy, with hidden woe, will lurk
In depth of pleasantness. Yet will ye rue
That laxity — a death. Defeat the foe! —
A task to which the bold alone are equal.

What a soul may earn is on its own account,
Nor doth any laden bear another's load.
So the hill of high attainment shall you mount
Who to Allah gladly pay what you have owed.

Daily task-performance ever paramount,
Grace of the Creator only as your goad,
Avid be your labor-love, a flowing fount.
Happily the reaper gathers what he sowed.

15.

Lyrical Response to Verses from Sura 7 "The Heights"

42. But (as for) those who believe and do good works — We tax not any soul beyond its scope — Such are rightful owners of the Garden. They abide therein.

43. And We remove whatever rancour may be in their hearts. Rivers flow beneath them. And they say: The praise to Allah, Who hath guided us to this. . . .

Tranquil be those who gladly do good deeds:
"We tax not any soul beyond its scope."
The rightful owner of the Garden heeds
High-minded impulse, and abides in hope.

Because the expectation suits the needs
Of humans who with vision-limits cope,
Great is the gain to which intention leads
When we with wiser guide ascend the slope.

Whatever rancor dwell in weary heart
Will be removed; that promise, granted all,
Lightens the load for those whom tasks appall

Which they, too hard self-lashed, in vain may start
And cannot finish. Calm, not conscience-dart,
For these. Feel Eden-rivers rise and fall...

16.

Lyrical Response to Verses from Sura 7 "The Heights" and Sura 62 "The Congregation"

7:156. . . . HE said: . . . My mercy embraceth all things, therefore I shall ordain it for those who ward off (evil) and pay the poor-due, and those who believe Our revelations;

157. Those who follow the messenger, the Prophet who can neither read nor write, whom they will find described in the Torah and the Gospel (which are) with them.

. . . . .

62:2. He it is Who hath sent among the unlettered ones a messenger of their own, to recite unto them His revelations and to make them grow, and to teach them the Scripture and Wisdom, though heretofore they were indeed in error manifest,

3. Along with others of them who have not yet joined them. He is the Mighty, the Wise.

. . . Muhammad must be ummī *so that the "inlibration," the revelation of the Divine Word in the Book, can happen without his own intellectual activity, as an act of grace; for as Hallaj (d. 922) says in his comparison of the Prophet with Iblis: "He withdrew from his own power by saying: 'In Thee I turn and in Thee I walk.'" (Annemarie Schimmel,* And Muhammad Is His Messenger, *72)*

> Muhammad was unlettered or *ummī.*
> No clutter of the intellect would claim
> The plain Proclaimer of the Holy Name.
> He would transmit in perfect purity
>
> The freshet-water of the depth, not frame
> A convoluted concept. Quibble-free,
> Unquelled outspilled the melody that came
> Of the great Cave Recital. Thus would he,
>
> Gabriel-aided, to his own convey,
> Unhindered in his telling, ev'n as they,
> Direct and lightning-bright, the higher way
>
> To make them grow. Those equal to the test,
> Though heretofore in error manifest,
> Felt heart by heaven cleansed within the breast.

17.

Lyrical Response to a Verse from Sura 7 "The Heights"

---

57. And He it is Who sendeth the winds as tidings heralding His mercy, till, when they bear a cloud heavy (with rain), We lead it to a dead land, and then cause water to descend thereon and thereby bring forth fruits of every kind. Thus bring We forth the dead. Haply ye may remember.

What kind of strength was in that soil devoid of rain?
One heard a muted call, whereto the storm cloud sped.
It was not null, it was but numb, laid low by pain.
Haply ye may recall. Thus bring We forth the dead.

A desert in the long-forsaken soul had lain
Awaiting, hearkening, the One to whom it pled
Bravely for grace, remembering great ancient gain.
Haply ye may recall. Thus bring We forth the dead.

The cloud, alarming-proud, from out the ocean main
Awoke in thunder-drum and raising up his head
Arose in gray, the kingly herald of spring grain.
Haply ye may recall. Thus bring We forth the dead.

With message of a mercy, bursting from the strain
Of eagerness to aid the famished, it had fed
The aching ravin of the quaking barren plain.
Haply ye may recall. Thus bring We forth the dead.

Heaven would nourish earth, and all the sacred train
Of spirits in the wind wove wreaths when they were wed —
Crowns out of rainbow made to celebrate the twain.
Haply ye may recall. Thus bring We forth the dead.

The land bore fruit. With ample banquet entertain
Crowds whom the loving ministers to Allah led!
Abundant be your gifts! He lives, whom woe had slain.
Haply ye may recall. Thus bring We forth the dead.

In seven days were made what never more shall wane
Should we but trust what life made rise from mortal bed.
Stalwart and pure our love, steady and free of stain.
Haply ye may recall. Thus bring We forth the dead.

18.

Lyrical Response to Verses from Sura 7
"The Heights"

---

199. Keep to Forgiveness (O Muhammad), and enjoin kindness. . . .

200. And if a slander from the devil wound thee, then seek refuge in Allah. Lo! He is Hearer, Knower.

201. Lo! those who ward off (evil), when a glamour from the devil troubleth them, they do but remember (Allah's guidance) and behold them seers!

Keep to forgiveness, O Muhammad! Kindliness command:
Let fountain-sounding lavishness abound throughout the land.
Should some be troubled by a jinn with rampant glamour-leers,
If they remember Allah's guidance, then behold them seers!

Keep to forgiveness, O Muhammad! Kindliness proclaim,
And love below, above, let flow to glorify His name.
Should some forget to chasten haste for fame's embrace and cheers,
If they remember Allah's guidance, then behold them seers!

Keep to forgiveness, O Muhammad! Kindliness require:
Wonderful the design whereby we brothers' love desire.
Should some, distraught or wanton, feel enfolded in their fears,
If they remember Allah's guidance, then behold them seers!

Keep to forgiveness, O Muhammad! Kindliness enjoin:
Pardon will still hostilities that lover-pearls purloin.
Should some, defending fortresses that fall, rejoin with jeers,
Help them remember Allah's guidance, and behold them seers!

Keep to forgiveness, O Muhammad! Kindliness implore:
Mutual comprehension opens wide the Heaven-door.
Who naught can hear but foes within, unstoppèd be their ears.
For if they once gain pardon-guidance, then behold them seers.

Keep to forgiveness, O Muhammad! Kindliness attain,
Returning good for ill, let loss of pride be spirit-gain.
The graying sky of hate the grace-full sun of loving clears:
Forgiveness be the guide unblinding minds, creating seers.

19.

Lyrical Response to a Verse from Sura 8
"Spoils of War"

---

11. . . . He made the slumber fall upon you as a reassurance from Him and sent down water from the sky upon you, that thereby He might purify you, and remove from you the fear of Satan, and make strong your hearts and firm (your) feet thereby.

He made the slumber fall upon you, reassuring
The mind and body of their peace, and water sent
To purify and cool you with the element
Of tranquil flowing life-endowing dew enduring:

Fear of the adversarial removing far,
He bade be strong your hearts and firm your feet thereby.
Within you virile inspiration-strength will lie,
Inwardly lighted as by Venus, evening star.

The battles of today are not like those of old.
Mental acuity, steady, rewards the bold
Combatting apathy in the defense of our

Siblings with blood of red or green. Upon this pow'r
Depends the continuity of earthly life!
Struggle for that! It is the only moral strife.

20.

Lyrical Response to Verses from Sura 12
"Joseph"

---

30. And women in the city said: The ruler's wife is asking of her slave-boy an ill deed. Indeed he has smitten her to the heart with love. We behold her in plain aberration.

31. And when she heard of their sly talk, she sent to them and prepared for them a cushioned couch (to lie on at the feast) and gave to every one of them a knife and said (to Joseph): Come out unto them! and when they saw him they exalted him and cut their hands, exclaiming: Allah Blameless! This is not a human being. This is no other than some gracious angel.

32. She said: This is he on whose account ye blamed me. I asked of him an evil act, but he proved continent, but if he do not my behest he verily shall be imprisoned, and verily shall be of those brought low.

33. He said: O my Lord! Prison is more dear than that unto which they urge me, and if Thou fend not off their wiles from me I shall incline unto them and become of the foolish.

34. So his Lord heard his prayer and fended off their wiles from him. Lo! He is Hearer, Knower.

> Potiphar's wife Zuleika had been caught
> Seeking to tempt her slave-youth captive. Now
> She'd brazen out her boldness, anyhow.
> For she had planned a lesson to be taught
>
> To jealous friends: "And what would *you* have done?
> Look at the man, could you resist him? See,
> You couldn't hold your fruit knives — clumsily
> You've cut your fingers. Love for such a one —
>
> Can it be blamed? I won't give up, not I!"
> Then turned aside pale Joseph, with a sigh,
> Praying, "O Lord, I'd rather be in jail."
>
> Allah, whose grace and favor never fail,
> Could sympathize and fended off their wiles.
> Godliness aids whom fate in vain beguiles.

21.

Lyrical Response to Verses from Sura 13
"The Thunder"

22. Such as persevere in seeking their Lord's countenance and are regular in prayer and spend of that which We bestow upon them secretly and openly, and overcome evil with good. Theirs will be the sequel of the (heavenly) Home,

23. Gardens of Eden which they enter, along with all who do right of their fathers and their helpmeets and their seed. The angels enter unto them from every gate,

24. (Saying): Peace be unto you because ye persevered. Ah, passing sweet will be the sequel of the (heavenly) Home.

We enter unto them by every gate of sense
Who evil overcome with good, so angels say.
Who aided parents, husband, wife, or children, they
Have led a life whose implications are immense.

Because you persevered, be peace your recompense,
The garden that you enter: pleasant winds will play
Near heaven-meadow, heart-glow mirroring the ray
Of Allah's tranquil face that tempers turbulence.

Ah, peace be unto you because ye persevere.
Ah, passing sweet the sequel of the heav'nly Home
Of Eden, no mere cloudy glimmer in the gloam

Of distant future vision, but already here —
An angel at the gate? No, three! Admit them, then.
Abraham, Sarah showed us how. Come in! Amen.

22.

Lyrical Response to a Verse from Sura 13
"The Thunder"

35. A similitude of the Garden which is promised unto those who keep their duty (to Allah): Underneath it rivers flow; its food is everlasting, and its shade; this is the reward of those who keep their duty, while the reward of disbelievers is the fire.

> Rewarded are believers in a Garden,
> Whereunder everlasting rivers flow,
> Where food is plenteous, cool shadows grow,
> Shelter engendered in a promised pardon.
>
> There souls, in peaceful evening, strolling go.
> But what, foreshadowed in a blood-fire blaze
> Waking, dispels the wet and whitened haze?
> It cries on the horizon, rising glow!
>
> O burning bush, the guiding, wise "I am"
> To Moses known, confirming Abraham
> Who, grateful, spoke with angels in his tent!
>
> What may the ones from sun and heaven rent
> Know of the striving fire, inciting minds?
> Baffled, the scholiast no answer finds.

23.

Lyrical Response to Verses from Sura 14
"Abraham"

---

24. Seest thou not how Allah coineth a similitude: A goodly saying, as a good tree, its root set firm, its branches reaching into heaven,

25. Giving its fruit at every season by permission of its Lord? . . . .

Seest thou not how Allah coineth a similitude:
A goodly saying, as a goodly tree, its root set firm,
                        Its branches reaching into heaven,
Giving its fruit at every season by permission of its Lord?

What came into my heart is nothing lesser than the time
When on the back of lightning rode the dazzled Prophet through
                        The highest heavens in a rapture
Seeing the giant-angel-laden Lote-tree at the utmost bound.

The godly metaphor of saying, rich prolific word,
Will show for every hearer forms, each view another fruit.
                        I do not scruple to conceive it:
The whole Creation may be seen as Allah's heaven-reaching Tree.

We dwell upon the middle boughs, a firm and central place;
The jinns within the jumble of the roots, bewildered they;
                        Gabriel and the greater angels
Above and overseeing, Michael showing splendid em'rald wings!

24.

Lyrical Response to Verses from Sura 15 "Al-Ḥijr"

---

26. Verily We created man of potter's clay of black mud altered,
27. And the Jinn did We create aforetime of essential fire.

> Iblis bragged, inactive sluggard, laxly puttered he and paltered,
> But the errors of that laggard will not merit even ire.
>
> 'Twas the Universal Life alone that never failed or faltered,
> Neither slumbering nor sleeping but excited by desire.
>
> Creativity that lives cannot be halted, held, or haltered,
> For the hands that hold the heaven than all humble homes are higher.
>
> May the makers of all music limned in hymns of awe and psaltered
> Be exalted in the lauded heav'n whereto they dare aspire!
>
> Truly We created man of potter's clay of black mud altered,
> And the Jinn did We create aforetime of essential fire.

25.

Lyrical Response to Verses from Sura 15 "Al-Ḥijr"

81. And we gave them Our revelations, but they were averse to them.

82. And they used to hew out dwellings from the hills, (wherein they dwelt) secure.

83. But the (Awful) Cry overtook them at the morning hour,

84. And that which they were wont to count as gain availed them not.

We gave them revelations, but they were averse to those.
They hewed out dwellings from the hills, wherein they dwelt secure.
The Awful Cry then overtook them at the morning hour,
And that which they were wont to count as gain availed them not,

The faction of the Rocky Tract. What could the tale disclose
If it were a similitude for us who would endure?
Deeming we're safe in rock-hewn rooms, we seize all earthly pow'r
And little think — so dulled and stunted is our nature-thought.

We have removed the hearts of hills; the mighty heads that rose
High in the twilight lopped, that we with plunder-will impure
Might brigand-like burn stolen coal, each meager seam to scour.
We take what cannot be replaced — what havoc have we wrought!

We damage habitats of caribou and bears, what grows
In icy climates perishing from sneaking heat. The poor
Folk of the world may die while our pollution-engines glow'r,
Their oil-filled maws defiant. Aye, the comfort that we sought

Abandoned us, our fever-greed the meanest of our foes.
Who love not others kill themselves. We our concerns immure
Within a stony selfhood-skull. Fallow of fruit and flow'r,
Our desert-minds desert us. Ills, by thoughtlessness begot!

26.

Lyrical Response to Verses from Sura 16
"The Bee"

65. Allah sendeth down water from the sky and therewith reviveth the earth after her death. Lo! herein is indeed a portent for a folk who hear.

66. And lo! in the cattle there is a lesson for you. We give you to drink of that which is in their bellies, from betwixt the refuse and the blood, pure milk palatable to the drinkers.

67. And of the fruits of the date-palm, and grapes, whence ye derive strong drink and (also) good nourishment. Lo! therein, is indeed a portent for people who have sense.

68. And thy Lord inspired the bee, saying: choose thou habitations in the hills and in the trees and in that which they thatch;

69. Then eat of all fruits, and follow the ways of thy Lord, made smooth (for thee). There cometh forth from their bellies a drink diverse of hues, wherein is healing for mankind. Lo! herein is indeed a portent for people who reflect.

Honey and milk and wine and water clear,
The first three telling of our fire, earth, air —
Kind elemental bounty everywhere!.
Indeed a portent for a folk who hear.

Exuberant the beauty we revere,
"Uber" is Latin "udder," and from there
Will come pure liquid overflowing fair.
Indeed a portent for a folk who hear.

Combs overbrimmed with honey will endear,
Much as a thankful heart new-freed from care
Pours antic, artless chanting unaware.
Indeed a portent for a folk who hear.

Wine of the palm and grape the heart will cheer
Taken in moderation, lending flair
To make a chosen moment yet more rare.
Indeed a portent for a folk who hear.

Water of life — it is of this that we're
Most chiefly made. For see! within we bear
Fountain and cistern, sweet symbolic pair.
Indeed a portent for a folk who hear.

Quaternity of nourishment — the sheer
Savoring of the flavors they prepare
Is for the body's mind a kind of prayer.
Indeed a portent for a folk who hear.

27.

Lyrical Response to a Verse from Sura 17 "The Children of Israel"

In the name of Allah, the Beneficent, the Merciful.

1. Glorified be He Who carried His servant by night from the Inviolable Place of worship to the Far Distant Place of Worship the neighbourhood whereof We have blessed, that We might show him of Our tokens! Lo! He, only He, is the Hearer, the Seer.

Tradition holds that on Buraq, a white-wing'd steed
The Prophet to Jerusalem from Mecca rode,
Thence to the highest heav'n, next Allah's lone abode.
To ready him for this incomparable deed,

Gabriel first removed the heart from out the chest
Of the blest Prophet, cleansing it with water pure
And holy, then replaced it, woundless, to ensure
Muhammad, like Isaiah, would endure God's test.

So the Sahih Bukhari *hádith* supplement
Reads. To the horse the Lord a lightning speed had lent,
Traversing all the heavens in a single night.

It is the finest metaphor of brightest thought
Whereby the mind to most exalted awe was brought,
Chosen to know of Allah's unapproachèd light.

28.

Lyrical Response to Verses from Sura 17 "The Children of Israel" and Sura 52 "The Mount"

17:11. Man prayeth for evil as he prayeth for good; for man was ever hasty.
. . . . .

52:48. So wait patiently (O Muhammad) for thy Lord's decree, for surely thou art in Our sight; and hymn the praise of thy Lord when thou uprisest,

49. And in the night-time also hymn His praise, and at the setting of the stars.

Men ask for evil as for good, for they
Were ever hasty, fain to fill the void
Hollowed by fear and hope with unalloyed
Wild fancy, while for might in pride they pray.

Far wiser, when you rise, to hail the day
With openness to what may be enjoyed.
Delicate food of selfhood will have cloyed.
Extend your Eden-soul instead, and say:

Illimitable godly space I praise,
Calm setting of the stars, befriending dawn,
Firelight that spiral nebulae will spawn,

Changed constellations' intermingling rays,
The solar system of each atom-sphere,
Sweet cleaving of a path by vision clear.

29.

Lyrical Response to Verses from Sura 17 "The Children of Israel"

23. The Lord hath decreed ... (that ye show) kindness to parents. If one of them or both of them attain old age with thee, say not "Fie" unto them nor repulse them, but speak unto them a gracious word.

24. And lower unto them the wing of submission through mercy, and say: My Lord! Have mercy on them both as they did care for me when I was little.

> The gifts within our nature are so amply granted,
> Long years are needed that they fully may unfold.
> Lower submission's wing to parents who are old:
> To them, so generous, let mercy not be scanted.
>
> They sowed a seed of light and nourished it when planted:
> A smile of sun-warmth, and the hidden tears untold
> They shed in sweet concern bespoke deep moral gold;
> Water of life, their grace, unstintingly decanted.
>
> They cared for me when I was little — how they cared!
> Without that daily bounty, kindly favor shared,
> What would I have become, beswept by winds of fate?
>
> Godlike their nourishing, in early times and late.
> Shelter them both in peace: your life and length of days
> You owe to these, their solar generative rays.

30.

Lyrical Response to Verses from Sura 19 "Mary"

---

19. He said: I am only a messenger of thy Lord, that I may bestow on thee a faultless son.

20. She said: How can I have a son when no mortal hath touched me, neither have I been unchaste?

21. He said: So (it will be). Thy Lord saith: It is easy for Me. And (it will be) that We may make of him a revelation for mankind and a mercy from Us, and it is a thing ordained.

22. And she conceived him, and she withdrew with him to a far place.

. . . . .

27. Then she brought him to her own folk, carrying him. They said: O Mary! Thou hast come with an amazing thing. . . .

29. Then she pointed to him. They said: How can we talk to one who is in the cradle, a young boy?

30. He spake: Lo! I am the slave of Allah. He hath given me the Scripture and hath appointed me a Prophet,

31. And hath made me blessed wheresoever I may be, and hath enjoined upon me prayer and alms-giving so long as I remain alive,

32. And (hath made me) dutiful toward her who bore me, and hath not made me arrogant, unblest.

33. Peace on me the day I was born, and the day I die, and the day I shall be raised alive!

34. Such was Jesus, son of Mary. . . .

> We knew the youth, of tender years, in temple spoke,
> And later, with a strength born of authority.
> Here we may hearken to a cradle homily
> With precepts taken much to heart, not hard the yoke

Of rules instilled which to fulfil would be his goal.
Charity, duty, prayer; in dying and when born,
Peace, ever peace the lesson, that prophetic morn.
Blessèd, not arrogant. A humbled, hallowed soul.

Best mother: woman with a greater grandeur graced
(For Islam finds her famed in heaven, ever chaste)
Than any but the others of the Perfect Four:

Asiya, spouse of Pharaoh during Moses' life;
Fàtima and Khadija, daughter and first wife
Of wise Muhammad — honored all, for evermore.

31.

Lyrical Response to Verses from Sura 23 "The Believers"

---

109. Lo! there was a party of My slaves who said: Our Lord! We believe, therefor forgive us and have mercy on us for Thou art best of all who show mercy;

110. But ye chose them for a laughing-stock until they caused you to forget remembrance of Me, while ye laughed at them.

111. Lo! I have rewarded them this day forasmuch as they were stedfast; and they verily are the triumphant.

112. He will say: How long tarried ye in the earth, counting by years?

113. They will say: We tarried but a day or part of a day. Ask of those who keep count!

114. He will say: Ye tarried but a little if ye only knew.

> The lovingly triumphant keep the time in view.
> 'Tis no swift river that will sweep us all away;
> We give it shape with what we sing, and make, and say.
> *Ye tarried but a little if ye only knew.*

> Attitudes toward the time we travel with are two:
> Laving, the lazy flow of waves that gaily play
> May bathe a soul that slowly floats within their sway.
> *Ye tarried but a little if ye only knew.*

> Yet we awoke to work when brisker winds that blew,
> Blustering, clove with cold the ruddy summer day,
> Announcing, raw, the close of August roundelay.
> *Ye tarried but a little if ye only knew.*

> Music is time alert with heartbeat driving through
> The psalmer's airy art that sculpts the winding way
> We ramble in the world past weald and bank and brae.
> *Ye tarried but a little if ye only knew.*

Yet pressing is the task we're planted here to do:
Harvest requires the hardy farmer hardly stray,
Preparing earth for rainwashed birth in long-sought ray.
Ye tarried but a little if ye only knew.

Heart-measure, tuned to sun and moon, will send the clue:
Our bright chaosmic blood that night will not affray
Lent rightful pace to Adam's race of reddened clay.
Ye tarried but a little if ye only knew.

From music of the Sons of God we take our cue.
In azure blaze they choired an Everlasting Yea
Unto the Guide who made the life that in them lay.
Ye tarried but a little if ye only knew.

32.

Lyrical Response to a Verse from Sura 24
"Light"

---

35. Allah is the Light of the heavens and the earth. The similitude of His light is as a niche wherein is a lamp. The lamp is in a glass. The glass is as it were a shining star. (This lamp is) kindled from a blessed tree, an olive neither of the East nor of the West, whose oil would almost glow forth (of itself) though no fire touched it. Light upon light. Allah guideth unto His light whom He will. And Allah speaketh to mankind in allegories, for Allah is Knower of all things.

Even as Milton claimed Isaiah's tale had shown
God touches with his holy flame the lips of whom
He chooses, here Muhammad's burning words illume
The miracle of grace whose ways may not be known.

An olive that from out no worldly ground had grown
Gave oil that would appear to hold in little room
Self-generated light that might disperse the gloom
And amplified by lamp of glass would starlight own.

The light of heav'n and earth is the creative will
Which as a tree from seed will ramify and fill
The eyes with fire of life, the voice with joy of love,

The mind with drive to write, the heart with panting beat,
The legs with will to dance, the hands to clap, the heat
Of blood-sunned hymn to chant and thank the One above.

33.

Lyrical Response to Verses from Sura 25
"The Criterion"

---

63. The (faithful) slaves of the Beneficent are they who walk upon the earth modestly, and when the foolish ones address them answer: Peace; . . .

67. And those who, when they spend, are neither prodigal nor grudging; and there is ever a firm station between the two; . . .

72. And those who will not witness vanity, but when they pass near senseless play, pass by with dignity.

> The faithful slaves of the Beneficent are they
> Who walk upon the earth in modesty, and when
>   The foolish ones address them answer: Peace.
>
> Brave are the trusting on the long and steadfast way
> Valiant in faithful action vital unto men:
>   The brighter eye will make the mocker cease.
>
> Rule then yourself, and want no other kind of sway
> But that exampled by the taller mind, which then
>   The bent from rampant madness can release.
>
> Be neither prodigal nor grudging, nor delay
> In giving needed alms, and giving alms again,
>   Calm, as a policy, not with caprice.
>
> Witness not vanity, but viewing senseless play
> Unheeding, pass it by in dignity, nor pen
>   Thinking in trivial cell: let depth increase.

34.

Lyrical Response to Verses from Sura 26 "The Poets" and Sura 33 "The Clans"

26:224. As for poets, the erring follow them.

225. Hast thou not seen how they stray in every valley,

226. And how they say that which they do not?

227. Save those who believe and do good works, and remember Allah much, and vindicate themselves after they have been wronged. . . .

. . . . .

33:45. O Prophet! Lo! We have sent thee as a witness and a bringer of good tidings and a warner.

46. And as a summoner unto Allah by His permission, and as a lamp that giveth light.

We have sent thee as a witness and a bringer of good tidings and a warner.
And a summoner to Allah by His granting, and a lamp that giveth light.

Yet Muhammad is no god, nor was: Gabriel-aided Reader and a Servant.
It is He who lights the way, with starry flame by the enkindling Pow'r
    endowed.

As for poets, though they stray in every valley overspread by wings of
    eagles,
They are not without the strength to do good works, recalling Allah's eye
    when wronged.

By the spark that leaps, and wholly warmth-enheartened with an empathy-
    arousal
Will the hearer of a sky-enlightened air conceive in lifetime-widened space.

Warning souls of gates untimely shut, of window-eyes benighted to the
    lightning,
Yet a bringer of the wander-shine of comets with their wild eccentric fire,

Yes! the poets hear the Prophet and may join him in the errand of rejoicing.
Let their works, not by their lives belied, but pouring forth a psalmer-virtue,
    soar!

35.

Lyrical Response to Verses from Sura 27 "The Ant"

7. (Remember) when Moses said unto his household: Lo! I spy afar off a fire; I will bring you tidings thence, or bring to you a borrowed flame that ye may warm yourselves.

8. But when he reached it, he was called, saying: Blessed is Whosoever is in the fire and whosoever is round about it! And glorified by Allah, the Lord of the Worlds!

9. O Moses! Lo! it is I, Allah, the Mighty, the Wise.

10. And throw down thy staff! But when he saw it writhing as it were a demon, he turned to flee headlong, (but it was said unto him): O Moses! Fear not! Lo! the emissaries fear not in my Presence,

11. Save him who hath done wrong and afterward hath changed evil for good. And lo! I am Forgiving, Merciful.

For Moses, looking at the warming fire,
Wherein the mighty Lord of Worlds (be blest),
Warning, appeared in glory, was a test:
"Throw down thy staff!" Cast off your own desire:

Bow to the power of the sacred flame!
The rod was wriggling as a demon-jinn,
Revealing what the leader found within:
Self, twisting in the memory of shame.

He'd killed a man, and he had been forgiven,
Yet was that writhing mind by lightning riven.
Allah the wrathful rebel-urge would quell,

Knowing the need to quench potential hell.
Don't kill, forgive! Though you with strength have striven,
Conquer that rock-hard will. And find a well.

36.

Lyrical Response to Sura 27
"The Ant"

---

16. And Solomon was David's heir. And he said: O mankind! Lo! we have been taught the language of birds, and have been given (abundance) of all things. This surely is evident favour.

17. And there were gathered together unto Solomon his armies of the jinn and humankind, and of the birds, and they were set in battle order;

18. Till, when they reached the Valley of the Ants, an ant exclaimed: O ants! Enter your dwellings lest Solomon and his armies crush you, unperceiving.

19. And (Solomon) smiled, laughing at her speech, and said: My Lord, arouse me to be thankful for Thy favour wherewith Thou hast favoured me and my parents, and so do good that shall be pleasing unto Thee, and include me in (the number of) thy righteous slaves.

As bird, ant, jinn — inhabitants of air, earth, fire —
In divers tongues by pow'r of the Divinity
Sing in the mind of him that hears their mighty choir,
Let me *do good that shall be pleasing unto Thee.*

That God a scryer and a servant may inspire
To aid in every labor heaven-favor saves,
Guide me to find my life merged with the light that's higher.
Include me in the number of thy righteous slaves.

A steward, in pursuit of duty, I'll not tire
Until beneath the sun all life as one I see.
Bird, ant, and jinn; pipe, timbrel, organ, flute and lyre,
Choral, *do good that shall be pleasing unto Thee.*

With drumming heartbeat pump, with neural spark and wire,
I dance and leap and clap and speak with light that laves,
Daring, in daily praise, to lavish love-desire.
Include me in the number of thy righteous slaves.

The bird will sail in air, the ant will ply the mire,
The jinn in flame alembicates an alchemy,
And I, their sibling — may I magnify our Sire
And so do good that shall be pleasing unto Thee.

I antlike build, I birdlike fly, the speeding spire
Of rising flame I jinnlike feel, the tidal waves
Climb in my veins, each breaker flung up far, a flyer —
Include me in the number of thy righteous slaves.

O Sabbath of my soul, in angel-eagle gyre
Let me ascend in hymn, omnific melody,
That I may blend with all that lauding lines require
And so do good that shall be pleasing unto Thee.

37.

Lyrical Response to Verses from Sura 28 "The Story" and Sura 66 "Banning"

28:6. And We inspired the mother of Moses, saying: Suckle him and, when thou fearest for him, then cast him into the river and fear not nor grieve. Lo! We shall bring him back unto thee and shall make him (one) of Our messengers.

8. And the family of Pharaoh took him up, that he might become for them an enemy and a sorrow. Lo! Pharaoh and Haman and their hosts were ever sinning.

9. And the wife of Pharaoh said: (He will be) a consolation for me and for thee. Kill him not. Peradventure he may be of use to us, or we may choose him for a son. And they perceived not.

66:11. And Allah citeth an example for those who believe: the wife of Pharaoh when she said: My Lord! Build for me a home with thee in the Garden, and deliver me from Pharaoh and his work, and deliver me from evildoing folk. . . .

Traditional it is to see the two as one:
The wife who viewed in Moses an adopted son
And she that knew of God, by Pharaoh unperceived,
And so example showed of those who have believed.

Setting the lines together takes me to the thought
Of what redemption, what delight the baby brought —
That Pharaoh's wife in tender love might thus be moved
To know him for a solace true. And so he proved.

Behold her gazing, rapt, into the infant's eyne
From which a double light into her own would shine
Prelusive of the twofold ray that all would see

When, after being granted the Commandments, he
Descended to the people from the Holy Mount.
Source of new life, the Law — their freedom and their fount.

38.

Lyrical Response to Verses from Sura 34 "Saba"

---

12. And unto Solomon (We gave) the wind, whereof the morning course was a month's journey and the evening course a month's journey, and We caused the fount of copper to gush forth for him, and (We gave him) certain of the jinn who worked before him by permission of his Lord. . . .

13. They made for him what he willed: synagogues and statues, basins like wells and boilers built into the ground. Give thanks, O House of David! Few of My bondmen are thankful.

To Solomon We gave the wind, whose morning course
Was a month's journey and the evening one as well;
A fount of molten copper; and some jinn, their spell
Insuring that a fiery stream's undaunted force

Meant that machines would far outdo the desert horse.
Basins and boilers, new-found waters — who can tell
How Solomon in wisdom could the jinn compel?
Yet when the mind left heart behind, behold, remorse!

The bondmen were not thankful who in pride of might
Enswathed in mourning dawn, the evening crimson light
In Tophet-smoke of steel Behemoth — fearful sight!

Demon of death, the rude polluters' ill-used wealth
Turning our weal to hell, steals from the world its health,
Stirring up storm instead, relentlessly, in stealth.

39.

Lyrical Response to Verses from Sura 35
"The Angels"

---

18. Unto Allah is the journeying.
19. The blind man is not equal with the seer;
20. Nor is darkness (tantamount to) light;
21. Nor is the shadow equal with the sun's full heat.

If unto Allah is the journeying;
And blind ones are not equal with the seer;
Nor is the darkness tantamount to light;
Nor is the shadow equal with the sun's full heat,

Yet one who's lit by inner fire is king
Over the seven heav'ns within — a sphere
Enclosed, refreshed with brightened, wider sight
Of the embracing greater circle; rare and sweet

The tones to him awakened, listening,
Alert as fledgling eagle stirred, to hear
The whirling music which the bringers bright
Made but for minds new-moved by wing'd afflatus fleet.

Then unto Him the journey be our spring
In triple meaning: season, source, and sheer
Leap of a soaring toward the core of might:
The Sun and eye, alike, their kindred warmth will meet.

40.

Lyrical Response to Verses from Sura 38
"Ṣad"

---

18. . . . remember Our bondman David, lord of might. Lo! he was ever turning in repentance (toward Allah).

19. Lo! we subdued the hills to hymn the praises (of their Lord) with him at nightfall and sunrise,

20. And the birds assembled; all were turning unto him.

21. We made his kingdom strong and gave him wisdom and decisive speech.

Recall Our bondman David, in repentance ever turning.
Lo! We subdued the hills to hymn the praises of their Lord
With him at nightfall and at sunrise: and the birds assembled,
For all were turning unto him. We made his kingdom strong,

Giving him wisdom and decisive speech. The hillocks yearning
To laud the King of Glory leapt with all the springtime stored
Within their depth, tall palm-trees tossed their heads, high mountains
        trembled,
For all were turning unto him with awed and holy song.

At nightfall and at sunrise, dawn and twilight, with a burning
As of a fire of sacrifice the sun, His servant, poured
Rays of thanskgiving praising Him in rapture undissembled,
With clouds of heav'n by rainbow made resplendent lauded long.

When David played the ten-stringed harp he calmed the monarch, earning
The gratitude of Saul who then his demons dark abhorred
Quickly dismissed. From mental fetters freed, the king resembled
One to whom dignity and might of Allah's sons belong.

41.

Lyrical Response to a Verse from Sura 41 "Fuṣilat"

53. We shall show them Our portents on the horizons and within themselves until it will be manifest unto them that it is the Truth. Does not thy Lord suffice, since He is Witness over all things?

Portent — on the horizon, and within our being!
Think of the starry sky and inward moral law
Bestirring Kant to admiration and to awe.
Insight and outward vision: symbol-mode of seeing.

Ourizein meant to make a circle, drawn around
A space. Yet a horizon's what we're moving toward:
This bright unbordered aim the Muslim names the Lord.
Behold an asymptote, a goal, receding bound

Betokening Beyond-Unbounded. What we call
A world is but the Open, beckoning with all
That may await the walker onward. Wander tall.

So, too, Husserlian phenomenology:
Roamers within a move-inviting world are we,
Finite, horizon-drawn to an infinity.

42.

Lyrical Response to Verses from Sura 42 "Counsel"

---

5. Almost might the heavens above be rent asunder while the angels hymn the praise of their Lord and ask for forgiveness for those on the earth. Lo! Allah is the Forgiver, the Merciful.

. . . . .

22. . . . those who believe and do good works (will be) in flowering meadows of the Gardens, having what they wish from their Lord. This is the great preferment.

23. This it is which Allah announceth unto His bondmen who believe and do good works. Say (O Muhammad, unto mankind): I ask of you no fee therefor, save lovingkindness among kinsfolk. And whoso scoreth a good deed We add unto its good for him. Lo! Allah is Forgiving, responsive.

. . . . .

36. . . . and that which Allah hath is better and more lasting for those who believe and put their trust in their Lord,

37. And those who shun the worst of sins and indecencies and, when they are wroth, forgive. . . .

. . . . .

43. And verily whoso is patient and forgiveth — lo! that, verily, is (of) the stedfast heart of things.

> Patience and pardon — at the steadfast heart of things.
> Angels that Allah elevate in daily praise
> Pray that forgiveness' grace may penetrate with rays
> As of a parent Sun th' imploring soul that sings.
>
> Patience and pardon — at the steadfast heart of things.
> Almost the heaven might be rent asunder while
> Storms yet refresh, for after awe shines forth a smile
> For wildered strayers in their jinn-flamed journeyings.

Patience and pardon — at the steadfast heart of things.
Why do the fiery seraphs loud in clamor call,
"May favor-words ring out in highest heaven-hall"?
Enamored is the One of those he granted wings.

Patience and pardon — at the steadfast heart of things.
They that forgive will merit fourfold Eden-meed:
Of honey, water, milk, and wine the streams proceed,
The while each youth and maid festoon and ribbon flings.

Patience and pardon — at the steadfast heart of things.
Who do good works, beyond proportion their reward
From the All-Plentiful, All-Merciful, the Lord
Who is the Heart of Pardon and the King of Kings.

43.

Lyrical Response to Verses from Sura 42 "Counsel"

32. And of His portents are the ships, like banners on the sea;

33. If He will he calmeth the winds so that they keep still upon its surface — Lo! herein verily are signs for every stedfast grateful (heart). —

The ships upon the surface of the heaving sea
Rise with the current of the laws that bind the brave,
Rest with relief, the tranquil balance that they crave
Coming with craft that kens the currents wild that we

Who are a fluxile blended-sundered wonder-wave
Feel in our changing wind-flailed nature made to be
Extravagating, winding, and evadingly
Divided-unified, to lash and, whitened, lave

With foam-flash, in the moan of lonely ocean rave,
And in the tidal chains that shall constrain the free
By favor of an ageless ordinance to save,

When raging, from the wages of the madding spree
What crashing on the shoreline shatters all it gave,
Only to be reborn, awaking from the grave.

44.

Imitation of Verses from Sura 44
"Smoke"

10. But watch thou (O Muhammad) for the day when the sky will produce visible smoke

11. That will envelop the people. This will be a painful torment.

12. (Then they will say): Our Lord relieve us of the torment. Lo! we are believers.

13. How can there be remembrance for them, when a messenger making plain (the truth) had already come unto them,

14. And they had turned away from him and said: One taught (by others), a madman?

I had a vision of a gorgon-looking face;
Whether of man or woman, I no more could tell,
And from it seemed to come the suffering of hell,
A fevered agony that fate would not erase.

The hairs were clumped together as with oil or mire,
And gathered up to points with sparks of reddish rust,
Enwreathed within a wind replete with smoky dust,
Wide eyes repeating redness in their bloody fire.

'Twas Gaea's refugee, whose glare of desperation
Spoke of abandonment by guardians of life
Who had succumbed to raving greed and ego-strife,

So that pollution loomed the turbid world above,
With what in seven days had once been made in love
Turned to an under-sun, a lethal radiation.

45.

Lyrical Response to Verses from Sura 44
"Smoke"

---

51. Lo! those who kept their duty will be in a place secure

52. Amid gardens and water-springs,

53. Attired in silk and silk embroidery, facing one another.

54. Even so (it will be). And we shall wed them unto fair ones with wide, lovely eyes.

A cure for solitude was wanted in the skies.
Attire of broidered silk, a garden water-spring,
All dull and lusterless, until the lover sing.
We'll wed them unto fair ones with wide, lovely eyes.

Allah created life, that thus He might devise
Rippling encounters round, each raindrop water-ring
Enamored of another richly-patterned thing.
We'll wed them unto fair ones with wide, lovely eyes.

A mind is mirrored in another's wild surmise.
What's echoed isn't merely self, but pleasuring
The queen with sparkle dark who's heartening the king.
We'll wed them unto fair ones with wide, lovely eyes.

In mutual regard the smitten hearts are wise.
Blessèd who let reflections long past numbering
Endlessly fruitful multiply, smiled light-waves fling.
We'll wed them unto fair ones with wide, lovely eyes.

The comelier the gaze, the more it will comprise.
What's lovable is love, that bright encompassing
Wherein a world unfurls, and rays of light will wing.
We'll wed them unto fair ones with wide, lovely eyes.

Being itself is round, the seërs realize.
The wreathing crown of Now no boundary will bring.
But lonely self-enclosure is a hidden sting.
We'll wed them unto fair ones with wide, lovely eyes.

When gazes interlace, the love that underlies
The liquid life of each will strive unwearying
To seek out means to please, with willing wind to swing.
We'll wed them unto fair ones with wide, lovely eyes.

46.

Lyrical Response to Verses from Sura 46 "The Wind-Curved Sandhills" and Sura 72 "The Jinn"

46:29. And when We inclined toward thee (Muhammad) certain of the Jinn, who wished to hear the Qur'ân and, when they were in its presence, said: Give ear! and, when it was finished, turned back to their people, warning.

30. They said: O our people! Lo! we have heard a Scripture which hath been revealed after Moses, confirming that which was before it, guiding unto the truth and a right road.

31. O our people! respond to Allah's summoner and believe in Him. He will forgive you some of your sins and guard you from a painful doom.

72:14. And there are some among us [Jinn] who have surrendered (to Allah) and there some among us who are unjust. And whoso hath surrendered to Allah, such have taken the right path purposefully.

Ev'n as in Eden righteous drink the wine
That leaves no dregs or aftertaste or ache,
All worldly vintages above, and take
Only the spirit-lifting gift benign,

So too the Jinn, of pure, essential flame
Where is no smoke or ashen residue,
Are penetrated, all their being through,
By furor, climbing drive no weight can tame.

The paradisal glad symposiasts
Have proven virtue of a kind that lasts.
Wine, they will not misuse. The fiery Jinn,

Sublunary, mixed-motived, isn't pure
In wisdom always. Yet the loved allure
Of Sun awakened some. New lives begin.

47.

Lyrical Response to Verses from Sura 47 "Muhammad" and Sura 83 "Defrauding"

47:15. A similitude of the Garden which those who keep their duty (to Allah) are promised: therein are rivers of water unpolluted, and rivers of milk whereof the flavour changeth not, and rivers of wine delicious to the drinkers, and rivers of clear-run honey; therein for them is every kind of fruit, with pardon from their Lord. . . .

83:22. Lo! the righteous verily are in delight,

23. On couches, gazing,

24. Thou wilt know in their faces the radiance of delight.

25. They are given to drink of a pure wine, sealed,

26. Whose seal is musk — For this let (all) those strive who strive for bliss —

27. And mixed with water of Tasnîm,

28. A spring whence those brought near to Allah drink.

> Of the Pison, Gihon too,
> Havilah and Hiddekel,
> That the just in Eden view,
> Genesis to you will tell.
>
> Rivers four — similitude
> Of a bliss in fruitfulness.
> Yet Muhammad's are endued
> Richlier the wise to bless.
>
> Honey, water, wine, and milk
> Favor them who've striven well,
> Resting on brocaded silk
> By the Pison, Hiddekel.
>
> Water, honey, milk, and wine
> Lately saved, with seal of musk —
> By the Gihon they'll recline
> Drinking this, at Eden-dusk,

Mixed with water of Tasnîm,
Spring where these near Allah drink.
Lordly the reward would seem.
Let the strayers pray and think!

On the couches, with a gaze
Radiant in godly sight,
Grace-partakers lend amaze;
Have, by Havilah, delight.

Unpolluted are the streams;
Running clear, the honey sweet;
Purer milk than childlike dreams,
Chilled the wine in currents fleet.

Thus the ones are nourished here
Who have earned a pearl-reward,
And what chiefly will endear
Is a pardon from their Lord.

48.

Lyrical Response to a Verse from Sura 48
"Victory"

29. Muhammad is the messenger of Allah. And those with him are . . . merciful among themselves. Thou (O Muhammad) seest them bowing and falling prostrate (in worship) seeking bounty from Allah and (His) acceptance. The mark of them is on their foreheads from the traces of prostration. Such is their likeness in the Torah and their likeness in the Gospel — like as sown corn that sendeth forth its shoot and strengtheneth it and riseth firm upon its stalk, delighting the sowers. . . .

Torah and Gospel and Qur'an present
The one that bows before the Wind of Him
Who is the fiery Light of seraphim
As livened by that finer element.

So the sown corn will rise renewed, the root
With force instilled by tillage of the soil
Nourished by virtue of a worthy toil
Enlivening the verdant early shoot.

Torah and Gospel and Qur'an — three rings
Like those the fabler, then the playwright, sings.
Golden, they told a triply noble tale.

Bounty rewards the one who, ardent, bows
Before the Light and Wind that will arouse
The upright stalk to rise, that cannot fail.

49.

Lyrical Response to a Verse from Sura 49 "The Private Apartments"

13. O mankind! Lo! We have created you male and female, and have made you nations and tribes that ye may know one another. Lo! the noblest of you, in the sight of Allah, is the best in conduct. Lo! Allah is Knower, Aware.

Many have heard the tale of Babel Tower,
Raised to the heavens, fated to collapse.
More dirgeful than encouraging, perhaps,
The consequence appeared a loss of power:

Proliferating languages — a dower
Of miscommunications, mental traps?
Yet fertile curiosity enwraps
Our nature; differences let it flower!

We sowed in tears, but yet may reap in smiles.
Ill will, hostility instilled, beguiles
The narrow, the confined, the unaware.

Genders and nations are more loved, more fair
Each to the other in diversity.
Praised be the pluriverse the clear-eyed see!

50.

Lyrical Response to Verses from Sura 51
"The Winnowing of Winds"

---

15. Lo! those who keep from evil will dwell amid gardens and watersprings,
16. Taking that which their Lord giveth them; for lo! aforetime they were doers of good;
17. They used to sleep but little of the night,
18. And ere the dawning of each day would seek forgiveness.
19. And in their wealth the beggar and the outcast had due share.

Think of the blest of legend, lending light.
They heard the squirrel's heartbeat in the spreading branches,
The whirr of wheeling pinions glimpsed that leafy wind-gusts bear.

They used to sleep but little of the night,
And ere the dawning of each day would seek forgiveness.
And in their wealth the beggar and the outcast had due share.

Bacteria with molecules would write
Upon the water, whence men learned an atom language.
What does the mind require? A cipher summons them that dare.

Who binds the tide and guides the acolyte
Sings in the artery and sparks the neural system.
Green-blooded hymn-blade rises wind-bathed swaying in the glare.

Take in, upon the waning of the night,
The contrapuntal scheme competing calls are mapping,
The math of polyrhythmic swing and impulse everywhere.

An aide would help King David to incite
The lyre upon the midnight hour by ringing
A wakening alarm, for one had little time to spare.

Denys, by some called Areopagite,
Deemed for the Ultimate each metaphor was lacking —
But feel them choir as One in water, fire and earth and air!

51.

Lyrical Response to Verses from Sura 53
"The Star"

In the name of Allah, the Beneficent, the Merciful.

1. By the Star when it setteth,

2. Your comrade erreth not, nor is deceived;

3. Nor doth he speak of (his own) desire.

4. It is naught save an inspiration that is inspired,

5. Which one of mighty powers hath taught him,

6. One vigorous; and he grew clear to view

7. When he was on the uppermost horizon.

8. Then he drew nigh and came down

9. Till he was (distant) two bows' length or even nearer,

10. And He revealed unto His slave that which he revealed.

11. The heart lied not (in seeing) what it saw.

12. Will ye then dispute with him concerning what he seeth?

13. And verily he saw him yet another time

14. By the lote-tree of the utmost boundary,

15. Nigh unto which is the Garden of Abode.

The evening guiding star will fall, and rise at dawn,
To symbolize the Prophet, weakened, later strong —
When Allah's righteous slave, your comrade, after long
Struggle, by inspiration saved, the jinn-fear gone,

Absorbed immortal force of one that filled the sky,
Towering from the uppermost horizon, down —
Two bows' length only distant in his pow'r — the crown
Of healing coming to bestow from Him on high.

Believe the heart lied not in seeing what it saw!
Not broken, no! renewed — bent low in fright and awe,
He rose, and rose again! — this time in heav'n to see

The lote-tree set beside the utmost boundary:
It bore no jujube-drupe, but ah! the lightsome load
Of giant angels, by the Garden of Abode.

52.

Lyrical Response to Verses from Sura 54
"The Moon"

In the name of Allah, the Beneficent, the Merciful.

1. The hour drew nigh and the moon was rent in twain.

2. And if they behold a portent they turn away and say: Prolonged illusion.

Now, when the hour drew nigh, the moon was rent in twain.
The parting of the sea, the tearing of the veil
Appear in Moses', Jesus' Bible wonder tale.
Portent is not illusion for a soul in pain.

Often the deepest are the hardest to explain.
Some view Muhammad as the *mim*, sun-letter sphere.
Two crescent *nun*s are made after the splitting; cheer
Descending from the numerology — as rain

On desert. Yet it *isn't* happy, not to me —
Dividing of the moon in white fragility.
I feel an omen of innumerable woes,

As in a dream that from the heart of darkness rose.
Interpreters will argue, others will demur.
Riven! What plangent anguish in the plight of her!

53.

Lyrical Response to Verses from Sura 55
"The Beneficent"

46. But for him who feareth the standing before his Lord there are two gardens. . . .

56. Therein are those of modest gaze, whom neither man nor jinni will have touched before them,

57. Which is it, of the favours of your Lord, that ye deny?

58. (In beauty) like the jacynth and the coral-stone.

59. Which is it, of the favours of your Lord, that ye deny?

60. Is the reward of goodness aught save goodness?

61. Which is it, of the favours of your Lord, that ye deny?

Which is it, of the favors of your Lord, that ye deny?
For blood and nerves and lymph and flesh and skin and hair contend
To give Him praise Who fashioned them. Raise then your hands up high:
Which is it, of the favors of your Lord, ye would commend?

The letters of the alphabet that mimic living forms
And in your lines delight and glide in flight and stretch and roll
And chant of the creation, rain and sun and cold and storms —
Which is it, of the favors of your Lord, ye would extol?

To speak of gladness and of woe in melismatic tones,
Those of the tapped tambour, the oaten flutes that wail and cry
In the Maulana mausoleum, vocal lauds and moans —
Which is it, of the favors of your Lord, ye'd magnify?

The honeysuckle sleeping on the oak, the flaunting rose,
Reveling sweet along the wind, the whitethorn loved in May
Opening eyes to greet the dawning brightness while it grows —
Which is it, of the favors of your Lord, ye would display?

Which is it, of the favors of your Lord, ye would disclose?
The seas and bays, the flaming constellations none can name,
The henna-fingered maid of daybreak-ray that faintly glows —
Which is it, of the favors of your Lord, ye would acclaim?

Which is it, of the favors of your Lord, ye would approve?
The comets that eccentric whirl, the wombing heaven vault?
The loud prophetic trees wherethrough the roaring surf-winds move?
Which is it, of the favors of your Lord, ye would exalt?

Lulling the dreaming mind to captivate the raptured ear
Are thrush and linnet and the goldfinch, robin and the wren —
Which is it, of the favors of your Lord, ye would revere?
Within you starry worlds are stored, ye women and ye men!

54.

Lyrical Response to Verses from Sura 56
"The Event"

---

10. And the foremost in the race, the foremost in the race:

11. These are they who will be brought nigh

12. In gardens of delight. . . .

15. On lined couches,

16. Reclining therein face to face.

17. There wait on them immortal youths

18. With bowls and ewers and a cup from a pure spring

19. Wherefom they get no aching of the head nor any madness. . . .

22. And (there are) fair ones with wide, lovely eyes,

23. Like unto hidden pearls,

24. Reward for what they used to do.

25. There hear they no vain speaking nor recrimination

26. (Naught) but the saying: Peace, (and again) Peace.

The foremost in the race will find he will have won
What never any athlete's known that's merely run
With tensing tendons and with glowing ruddy face,
Rival in energy to the ascending sun.

Such wonders of our youthful purpose have their place
Of honor, but the younger strivings interlace
With a more brave and rarer contest we begin:
Two selves contend — one lower, one of higher grace.

The foremost in the running is the one who'll win
By the outdistancing of an attractive twin
That, if not evil, yet is lacking in the zeal
Mustering like the call of prophecy within.

The one who beckons higher, to a goal ideal,
Reminds us of a jinn enlightened, whom the real
Wisdom of Allah had enwhirled and turned his mind
Round from its former course — Ezekiel's fiery wheel.

The newly tranquil valiant victor now will find
No aching of the head by madness that can blind,
Rather will drink from ewer of a purer spring
And rest upon a sofa soft and silken-lined.

He with a deep-souled maid an Eden-hymn will sing
The while above them nightingales may lightly wing.
No empty speaking or recrimination. Kind
To them who merit heav'n with kindness, heaven's King.

55.

Lyrical Response to Verses from Sura 57
"Iron"

20. Know that the life of the world is only play, and idle talk, and pageantry, and boasting among you, and rivalry in respect of wealth and children; as the likeness of vegetation after rain, whereof the growth is pleasing to the husbandman, but afterward it drieth up and thou seest it turning yellow, then it becometh straw. . . .

21. Race one with another for forgiveness from your Lord and a Garden whereof the breadth is as the breadth of the heavens and the earth. . . .

23. That ye grieve not for the sake of that which hath escaped you, nor yet exult because of that which hath been given. Allah loveth not all prideful boasters,

24. Who hoard and who enjoin upon the people avarice. . . .

Two plantings huge the verses paint. The one will bloom to fade:
Pageantry, play, and idle talk, by rivalry made vain,
Seeming the like of greening vegetation after rain,
Will wane and wither, humble straw, the husbandman dismayed.

Boasting among you? Competition with respect to wealth?
Mere self-promotion of an image, by the self adored?
Nay, race with one another for forgiveness from your Lord! —
An Eden-land new-animated by a wholeness-health.

The breadth of it is as the breadth of heavens and the earth,
For the receptive mind and heart the bounty of the world
Inhale and then breathe out, in swift surrounding life enswirled;
Wind taken in, a pulse of new arrival come to birth.

Those who enjoin upon the people ever-growing greed
And pride of sheer possession turn the freshened air to dust.
Accumulation is a prison-gloom; such roiling lust
Will blast the dew and spoil the leaf, the canker kill the seed.

How does the verdure that we seek enfold the earth and sky?
Mind-merger with our universe, in thankfulness and tears!
The life-charge of an atom, awed, the fervent soul reveres:
My body, hand — the sand of stars in One Almighty I.

Then grieve not ever for the loss of that which had escaped,
Nor yet exult in pride because of that which has been giv'n.
Nought counts but generosity, however you have striv'n
Molding your purposes to those the shining Eye had shaped.

56.

Lyrical Response to Verses from Sura 63
"The Hypocrites"

9. O ye who believe! Let not your wealth nor your children distract you from remembrance of Allah. Those who do so, they are the losers.

10. And spend of that wherewith We have provided you before death cometh unto one of you and he saith: My Lord! If only thou wouldst reprieve me for a little while, then I would give alms and be among the righteous.

Who live within the future only are the losers.
The present is your gift, and so repay it now.
The benefactions Allah granted show you how:
Reach out to those in need. To sluggard work-refusers

Teach: only life is wealth. Unmoving riches die,
Much as the carmine blood when stagnant turns to black.
The art of living well in Time will never lack
A fertile interaction of the tenses. Try

To activate the past with future aims in view.
Refreshed in purpose every moment, one more "you"
Is born, in life-stream blent of soul-identities,

The past regaining strength in present deeds that please.
The future moves the past to mean in present time.
Tenses regenerate in reason and in rhyme.

57.

Lyrical Response to a Verse from Sura 67
"The Sovereignty"

---

19. Have they not seen the birds above them spreading out their wings and closing them?
Naught upholdeth them save the Beneficent. Lo! He is Seer of all things.

Above the Himalàyas Asian geese can fly
From southern India one thousand miles a day
On thermal currents, bound for cold Tibet, where they
Will nest, then floating back, over those towers high.

That navigating skill can make the seër sigh
With wonder at the compass leading on their way
The calm, tan-feathered wings with borders white that sway
Tranquil. A more than man-wise calculating eye!

I write these words, my fingers floating over keys,
Propelled by apt synaptic neuron urgencies
Bestirred in mechanisms that extrinsecate

Quick-gliding, glinting impulse-wills that won't abate.
I trace a way upon the waiting paper white,
My hidden sextant guiding wingèd hands aright.

58.

Lyrical Response to Verses from Sura 68
"The Pen"

---

1. Nûn. By the pen and that which they write`(therewith)

2. Thou art not, for thy Lord's favour unto thee, a madman.

3. And lo! thine verily will be a reward unfailing.

4. And lo! thou art of a tremendous nature.

5. And thou wilt see and they will see

6. Which of you is the demented.

7. Lo! thy Lord is best aware of him who strayeth from his way, and He is best aware of those who walk aright.

8. Therefore obey not thou the rejecters

9. Who would have had thee compromise, that they may compromise.

. . .

47. Or is the Unseen theirs that they can write (thereof)?

48. But wait thou for thy Lord's decree, and be not like him of the fish, who cried out in despair.

49. Had it not been that favour from his Lord had reached him he surely had been cast into the wilderness while he was reprobate.

50. But his Lord chose him and placed him among the righteous.

51. And lo! those who disbelieve would fain disconcert thee with their eyes when they hear the Reminder, and they say: Lo! he is indeed mad;

52. When it is naught else than a Reminder to creation.

> Now by the pen I swear and what they write unwisely,
> You are not, for God's favor unto you, a madman.
> Behold, yours verily will be reward unfailing,
> And you and they will see which men are the demented.
> The Lord is best aware who strays, who walks directly,
> Therefore do not obey, distraught, the fond rejecters
> Who would that you might compromise, that they may do so.

Or is the Unseen theirs, that like to write about it?
Wait for the Lord's decree, not reft of hope as Jonah:
Had not God's favor reached the man, he were an outcast,
But being loved of Him was placed among the righteous.
The disbelievers disconcert you, crying, "Madman!"
Yet are your words but a Reminder to creation.

59.

Lyrical Response to Verses from Sura 73
"The Enshrouded One"

In the name of Allah, the Beneficent, the Merciful.

1. O thou wrapped in thy raiment!

2. Keep vigil the night long, save a little —

3. A half thereof, or abate a little thereof

4. Or add (a little) thereto — and chant the Qur'ân in measure.

5. For We shall charge thee with a word of weight.

6. Lo! the vigil of the night is (a time) when impression is more keen and speech more certain.

7. Lo! thou hast by day a chain of business.

8. So remember the name of thy Lord and devote thyself with a complete devotion —

9. Lord of the East and the West; there is no God save Him; so choose thou Him alone for thy defender —

10. And bear with patience what they utter, and part from them with a fair leave-taking.

11. Leave Me to deal with the deniers, lords of ease and comfort (in this life); and do thou respite them awhile.

> Wrapped in their raiment are the Prophet and the night.
> In each the tone of quiet sounds the ocean Truth.
> Shrouded as in a shell of ever-during youth
> A silence in the whorlèd human ear the light
>
> By vatic voice within and on the water sings.
> White shell: if it be wisely held, that we may hear
> The sea-like hymn, it amplifies our blood-rush clear
> Whose might of tide and current breakers' wave-surf brings.

Rèspite the guest with patience. Do thou but depart.
Night-shell of spirit let reveal unto the heart
A message of the East and West, a word of weight.

Let Man, who's born in freedom, work a grander fate.
May long-abiding comfort of a deep-drawn ease
Come from the night-accorded kingly mysteries.

60.

Lyrical Response to Verses from Sura 76
"Time" or "Man"

---

7. (Because) they perform the vow and fear a day whereof the evil is wide-spread,

8. And feed with food the needy wretch, the orphan and the prisoner, for love of Him, . . .

11. Therefor Allah hath warded off from them the evil of that day, and hath made them find brightness and joy;

12. And hath awarded them for all that they endured, a Garden and silk attire;

13. Reclining therein upon couches, they will find there neither (heat of) a sun nor bitter cold.

14. The shade thereof is close upon them and the clustered fruits thereof bow down.

15. Goblets of silver are brought round for them, and beakers (as) of glass

16. (Bright as) glass but (made) of silver, which they (themselves) have measured to the measure (of their deeds). . . .

19. There serve them youths of everlasting youth, whom, when thou seest, thou wouldst take for scattered pearls.

20. When thou seest, thou wilt see there bliss and high estate.

21. Their raiment will be fine green silk and gold embroidery. Bracelets of silver will they wear. Their Lord will slake their thirst with a pure drink.

Who *feed with food the needy wretch, the orphan and the prisoner,*
These will their Lord in time reward. Beakers of silver clear as glass
Filled with pure drink the pearl-bright youths for their delight around will
    pass,
While they on couches may recline, favored with fruits they would prefer.

Who *feed with food the needy wretch, the orphan and the prisoner,*
These by their deeds have measured out their later bliss in high estate.
Green silk and gold embroidery with silver bracelets them await;
Huge, the bejeweled Eden-blooms with silken color will concur.

Who *feed with food the needy wretch, the orphan and the prisoner,*
Tree-shade above is close to them and clustered fruits thereof bow down.
Nor burning sun nor bitter cold nor louring cloud on these will frown,
Nor harm the garden cardamom and cinnamon and nard and myrrh.

Who *feed with food the needy wretch, the orphan and the prisoner,*
They're blest with an eternal rest because they have performed the vow.
With kindliness and reverence the blessed youths to them will bow,
For these, each one, were like a sun to smile on seeds, a nourisher.

61.

Lyrical Response to Verses from Sura 84 "The Sundering" and Sura 101 "The Calamity"

84:16. Oh, I swear by the afterglow of sunset,

17. And by the night and all that it enshroudeth,

18. And by the moon when she is at the full,

19. That ye shall journey on from plane to plane.

101:4. A day when mankind will be as thickly-scattered moths

5. And the mountains will become as carded wool.

6. Then, as for him whose scales are heavy (with good works),

7. He will live a pleasant life.

I swear it by the sunset afterglow,
And by the night and all that it enshrouds,
And by the moon when she is at the full,
That you will journey on from plane to plane.

Behold! for to whatever realm ye go,
How dark soever heav'n may be with clouds
Abounding, or how deep the sea-tide pull,
Know that your wandering is not in vain.

Despair may pelt the soul with blinding snow,
Fiery frustration fill with jinns in crowds
The fevered brain, as of a pain-raged bull,
Yet shall the lover's high desire not wane.

When, with the storm-led force of evil foe,
Hordes of thick-scattered moth-men hell emprouds
Among the mountains rent as carded wool,
Who steer by heart-star will with Love remain.

62.

Lyrical Response to Verses from Sura 86 "The Morning Star"

1. *By the heavens and the Morning Star*

2. *— Ah, what will tell thee what the Morning Star is?*

3. *— The piercing Star!*

4. *No human soul but hath a guardian over it.*

5. *So let man consider from what he is created.*

6. *He is created from a gushing fluid*

7. *That issued from between the loins and ribs.*

The gushing fluid and the rising morning star,
The water and the fire, the fountain and the flame
Alembicate the alchemy from whence we came.
Yet potter's clay and air combine in what we are,

As the returning bird, new-flown here from afar
Sings to remind me right outside my window-frame.
Person and bird, in this allied, their song the same,
Love the like liquid and the sun-life none can bar.

The union in us all of unlike elements —
Behold the wonder known of old. In ancient tents
The tale was told of rainbow, flood, and Noah-dove

And then of Moses' blazing solar bush and of
The spirit wind that long before the world was made
Wafted on darkness while the jinns and angels prayed.

63.

Lyrical Response to Verses from Sura 88 "The Overwhelming"

8. *In that day other faces will be calm,*

9. *Glad for their effort past,*

10. *In a high garden*

11. *Where they hear no idle speech,*

12. *Wherein is a gushing spring,*

13. *Wherein are couches raised*

14. *And goblets set at hand*

15. *And cushions ranged*

16. *And silken carpets spread.*

17. *Will they not regard the camels, how they are created?*

18. *And the heaven, how it is raised?*

19. *And the hills, how they are set up?*

20. *And the earth, how it is spread?*

21. *Remind them, for thou art but a remembrancer,*

22. *Thou art not at all a warder over them.*

Glance at the gushing spring, the goblet, carpet spread
In silk; behold the camels, heaven, earth astir.
A warder art thou not, but a remembrancer.

Glad of their effort past, the just are comforted.
Fresh Garden-wine will they imbibe, that hearts prefer.
A warder art thou not, but a remembrancer.

Who pardon graver flaws by grace are garlanded.
Comely it is to love one's lot without demur.
A warder art thou not, but a remembrancer.

Like Moses, Jesus, and Muhammad, who were led
Along that road whereon the highest hopes concur,
A warder art thou not, but a remembrancer.

The heaven, hills are raised. Wills weary, flat, unfed
You may embrave, uplift with sweeping winds awhirr.
A warder art thou not, but a remembrancer.

High is the bright reward of him whose noble head
Shows lordly truths within, that awe and calm aver.
A warder art thou not, but a remembrancer.

When twilight over land a Sabbath shawl hath spread
Know then resplendent rest, sevenfold holier,
A warder being not, but a remembrancer.

64.

Lyrical Response to Verses from Sura 90
"The City"

8. Did We not assign unto him two eyes

9. And a tongue and two lips,

10. And guide him to the parting of the mountain ways?

11. But he hath not attempted the Ascent —

12. Ah, what will convey unto thee what the Ascent is! —

13. (It is) to free a slave,

14. And to feed in the day of hunger

15. An orphan near of kin,

16. Or some poor wretch in misery,

17. And to be of those who believe and exhort one another to perseverance and exhort one another to pity.

Jesus, Muhammad, Moses to the rise
Proved equal that such godly hearts command.
Each on an altar-mount not made by hand
Proclaimed the holy secret of the skies:

Only the willing friend knows the Ascent.
It is to feed an orphan, free a slave;
They the Ascent have known who gladly gave
Unto the wretched, and have pleasure lent.

Ascenders aid the strained to persevere.
To pity they will spur each other on,
Showing them hope who thought all grace long gone.

Gabriel in Muhammad's cave made clear
What Jesus, Moses, too upon the height
Revealed: the love of brothers, Allah-bright.

65.

Lyrical Response to Verses from Sura 91
"The Sun"

In the name of Allah, the Beneficent, the Merciful.
1. By the sun and his brightness,
2. And the moon when she followeth him,
3. And the day when it revealeth him,
4. And the night when it enshroudeth him,
5. And the heaven and Him who built it,
6. And the earth and Him who spread it,
7. And a soul and Him who perfected it
8. And inspired it (with conscience of) what is wrong for it and (what is) right for it.
9. He is indeed successful who causeth it to grow,
10. And he is indeed a failure who stunteth it.

Those in whom Soul grows high have magnified the Sun
Within; and, too, the one who stunted Sun-Soul fails.
Hear the similitude, and hearken. It entails
A doctrine that may rightly startle anyone.

Not-knowing is our veil. So night enwraps the earth.
Friendly are moon and planet that our minds attract;
Heaven, and world, and spirit — granted what they lacked,
Extended, lifted up, inspired by wisdom-birth.

The brightness in our eyes reflects the fiery star
That is the hidden soul. A darker solar blaze
Ilumines dream by night while reason guides our days.

The lighter, darker solar spheres, combining, are
Two forms of moral strength, which does not disappear
But varyingly works in worlds obscure and clear.

66.

Lyrical Response to Sura 93
"The Morning Hours"

In the name of Allah, the Beneficent, the Merciful.

1. By the morning hours

2. And by the night when it is stillest,

3. Thy Lord hath not forsaken thee nor doth He hate thee,

4. And verily the latter portion will be better for thee than the former,

5. And verily thy Lord will give unto thee so that thou wilt be content.

6. Did He not find thee an orphan and protect (thee)?

7. Did He not find thee wandering and direct (thee)?

8. Did He not find thee destitute and enrich (thee)?

9. Therefor the orphan oppress not,

10. Therefor the beggar drive not away,

11. Therefor of the bounty of thy Lord be thy discourse.

> Speak of Him in the brightened day.
> Once orphan, poor, and wide astray,
> New-fathered, now enriched, and found,
> Favored by One with kindness crowned.
>
> Tell of His pure and quiet might
> Who loosed the horses of the night
> Then led them back when dawn, still dim,
> Prophesied fire of seraphim.
>
> Sing of the rescuing of lost
> Wanderers by the whirlwind tossed
> That in sirocco and simoom
> Foretold, feared stern and certain doom.

Hymn in your heart the healing One
That with a mild and smiling sun
In love-enveloped aery space
Offered a grand and ample grace.

Seek out His image in the least,
And lead the famished to the feast.
Find the affrighted and alone
And bring them home, where light is sown.

Though luck be lost and fortunes fade,
Within this vale the soul is made.
The under-light will shine above.
Who has not suffered cannot love.

67.

Lyrical Response to Verses from Sura 94
"Solace"

In the name of Allah, the Beneficent, the Merciful.

1. Have We not caused thy bosom to dilate,

2. And eased thee of the burden

3. Which weighed down thy back;

4. And exalted thy fame?

Baihaqi-legacy far more will tell
Of the dilation of that holy breast.
Whereas three angels came, the faithfulest,
With aid for Abraham, it now befell

Three beings would approach the Prophet, then
Transport him to a mountaintop. The first
Applied the knife. Intestines he aspersed
With water, washed, replaced. The second, when

His friend had left, next clove the Prophet-heart,
Took out a blood-filled speck of black and threw
Away that fragment loathed. 'Twas Iblis' part.
He filled the organ with an essence new,

Restored it, and with cooling seal of light
Closed it. The calm spread out through joints and veins.
The third with angel-spell assuaged the pains,
Passing above the breast a hand of might.

The Prophet's benefactions would outweigh
Those of ten men. He heard the angel say,
"Fear you will never feel. If people knew
What heav'nly wealth has been prepared for you!"

The angel kissed his head, between the eyes;
And then all three flew up into the skies.
While Sarah, old, was told of coming birth,
The Prophet news would tell to sons of earth.

One *hádith* claims that he had Prophet been
While Adam in the mind of Allah lay,
Not made as yet of water and of clay.
Behold! the miracle that we have seen

Shows him reborn in holy agony
Through ministrations from the three above.
For without anguish in extremity
No son of Adam knows a human love.

68.

Lyrical Response to Sura 94
"Solace"

In the name of Allah, the Beneficent, the Merciful.

1. Have We not caused thy bosom to dilate,

2. And eased thee of the burden

3. Which weighed down thy back;

4. And exalted thy fame?

5. But lo! with hardship goeth ease,

6. Lo! with hardship goeth ease;

7. So when thou art relieved, still toil

8. And strive to please thy Lord.

Straightening up your back again,
After a burden borne, can please —
Deep breathing, free, relieving pain.
   With hardship goeth ease.

Lengthening of a well-stretched frame
Lends height, while strengthened symmetries
Portend a boldness bringing fame.
   With hardship goeth ease.

Extended effort, stronger stride,
More mental reaching — trying these,
We feel the life that will abide.
   With hardship goeth ease.

To labor by the sweat of brow
Is gift and gain. Our energies
Tower in strains that growth allow.
    With hardship goeth ease.

May passion-thunders not remain
Soft rumbling-low proclivities,
But pressure freed in freshened rain!
    With hardship goeth ease.

69.

Lyrical Response to Verses from Sura 96
"The Clot"

"the first of the Koran to be revealed"

1. Read: In the name of thy Lord who createth,

2. Createth man from a clot.

3. Read: And thy Lord is the Most Bounteous,

4. Who teacheth by the pen,

5. Teacheth man that which he knew not.

Creating from a clot and teaching by the pen...
The verses lead to think of sperm immixed with blood
And ink that's partly water. Fourfold is the flood
Of images of life that come together then:

With mind, heart, spirit, body unified we ken
The germinating life of writing. It is good
This kinship with our Author well be understood.
Disseminator-Gabriel no learned men

Sought out, but one unlettered. Yet, as happened when
Great Jacob conquered awe-filled might, though angel-lamed,
Muhammad, made to read, reciter ever-famed,

Was wrestled into victory and wrested from
Holy compulsion deep and lyric freedom. Come
To heav'n on lightning-steed, he triumphed yet again.

70.

Lyrical Response to Sura 97
"Power"

In the name of Allah, the Beneficent, the Merciful.

1. Lo! We revealed it on the Night of Power.

2. Ah, what will convey unto thee what the Night of Power is!

3. The Night of Power is better than a thousand months.

4. The angels and the Spirit descend therein, by the permission of their Lord, with all decrees.

5. (That night is) Peace until the rising of the dawn.

> The Night of Power is the Night of Peace;
> The angel Gabriel, whose name is Might,
> Stern wrestler-midwife on Reciting Night
> Forcing forth words till dawn, that meant release.
>
> The Power that compelled will never cease,
> Awe-full in darkness yet alluring-bright,
> Pre-sent and present and presaging flight,
> Parturient, whose labor is delight.
>
> The angels will descend with all decrees.
> Their strength will press the mind that it would please.
> A thousand months of absence matter less.
>
> Birthing within the only womb where dwell
> The yearning depths of holy loneliness,
> It hefts loud heaven out of silent hell.

71.

Lyrical Response to Sura 102
"Rivalry in Worldly Increase"

In the name of Allah, the Beneficent, the Merciful.

1. Rivalry in worldly increase distracteth you

2. Until ye come to the graves.

3. Nay, but ye will come to know!

4. Nay, but ye will come to know!

5. Nay, would that ye knew (now) with a sure knowledge!

6. For ye will behold hell-fire.

7. Aye, ye will behold it with sure vision.

8. Then, on that day, ye will be asked concerning pleasure.

Would that ye had brave wisdom, on deep vision based.
Let rivalry in worldly increase flee from you
So, later asked concerning pleasure, you won't view
A failing flame impure, strange mirror to be faced!

Those who are aiming at unholy goals have raced
Upward like tongues of greedy flame fed by untrue
Fuel, untrustable, corrupted — with a hue
Of cinder, not of ash, the glory-ore defaced.

How to discern the hell of low from higher fire
Of heaven? Vital is the flame of soul-desire
As in the bush beheld by Moses. Like a fount

Of water limpid, life-derived, the rush will mount
In sky-blue richness of a flute in liquid praise
With heart-warm art-borne words of Allah's works and ways.

72.

Lyrical Response to Sura 104
"The Traducer"

In the name of Allah, the Beneficent, the Merciful.

1. Woe unto every slandering traducer,

2. Who hath gathered wealth (of this world) and arranged it.

3. He thinketh that his wealth will render him immortal.

4. Nay, but verily he will be flung to the Consuming One.

5. Ah, what will convey unto thee what the Consuming One is!

6. (It is) the fire of Allah, kindled,

7. Which leapeth up over the hearts (of men).

8. Lo! it is closed in on them

9. In outstretched columns.

Who'd make himself a god by gathering great wealth
Is but a slandering traducer of the whole
Whereof the heav'ns intend he be a helpful part.
He that adores mere gain, consumer, is consumed.

Companionship and sharing are a nation's health,
While one who would become a hoarder-lord the role
Of plaguy parasite has taken on. Such art
At the dire fruit-tree of the greedy serpent loomed.

The open hand of generosity to stealth
And rabid acquisition is opposed. Your goal:
To feel the oneness of the light where life will start.
Said Allah, Let love be! So was the world illumed.

For common weal that must create a commonwealth
Requires no high estate be made of what one stole.
The warmth of brother-love be kindled in your heart
By Allah welcomed home where Eden rose-tree bloomed.

73.

Lyrical Response to Sura 108
"Abundance"

In the name of Allah, the Beneficent, the Merciful.

1. Lo! We have given thee Abundance;

2. So pray unto thy Lord, and sacrifice.

3. Lo! it is thy insulter (and not thou) who is without posterity.

The Prophet was derided; all his sons died young.
His daughter bore descendants; Fàtima would be
Among the heav'nly four in perfect sanctity
As well. Abundance? Let the taunter hold his tongue.

The latter lacked abundance in the spirit. This
Had amply been revealed in conduct mean and low.
Human or tree — 'tis by their fruits that we may know
The barren from the blest. The Prophet offered bliss.

The forms of mental plentitude may surely be
Properly called a many-fold posterity
(Including song, Qur'an-engendered poetry).

The Prophet we may praise for other sons — each deed
Of moral worth his progeny. Let hearers heed:
The wingèd word, wise work survive as light-born seed.

74.

Lyrical Response to Sura 113
"The Daybreak"

In the name of Allah, the Beneficent, the Merciful

1. Say: I seek refuge in the Lord of the Daybreak

2. From the evil of that which He created;

3. And from the evil of the darkness when it is intense,

4. And from the evil of blowers upon knots,

5. And from the evil of the envier when he envieth.

Benignity and mercy we implore
That when the morning rises cold and clear
So far as now the gold's an open door

Deeper enigmas of the world endear.
Sorceries of the body and the mind;
Of dark, bright; earth, air, water, flamy sphere;

Stream out, away, from spirit unconfined,
That we may stand, hymn-wing'd, on cloudy floor,
Our sight with crimson oriflammes aligned,

While wind sings in our heartstrings, oceans pour
Of light, which is the life that we adore.

75.

Lyrical Response to Sura 114 "Mankind"

In the name of Allah, the Beneficent, the Merciful.

1. Say: I seek refuge in the Lord of mankind,

2. The King of mankind,

3. The God of mankind,

4. From the evil of the sneaking whisperer,

5. Who whispereth in the hearts of mankind,

6. Of the jinn and of mankind.

This final, moving sura of the vast Qur'an
Calls on the Lord and King and God of humankind:
A refuge in the first embraving words we find.
In the symmetric second half we barely can

Maintain that faith entire without new strength infused.
For here the sneaking whisperer, who whispereth
In heart of man of clay and jinn of fire by breath
Of evil threatens, primal spirit that abused

Naïve delight of both aforetime, with a voice
Below the level of awareness, that to death
Led with a secretive and subtle serpent sting.

The sword that wards the life-tree ever severeth
One heart from others. Who won't love cannot rejoice,
Nor with the Sons of God the Sun of Glory sing.

PART 2

Lyrical Responses to the Qur'an
With Reference to Other Sources

76.

Lyrical Response to Sura 1
"The Opening" and a Goethe Quatrain

In the name of Allah, the Redeemer, the Merciful,

1. Praise be to Allah, Lord of the Worlds,

2. The Beneficent, the Merciful.

3. Owner of the Day of Judgment,

4. Thee (alone) we worship; Thee (alone) we ask for help.

5. Show us the straight path,

6. The path of those whom Thou hast favoured;

7. Not (the path) of those who earn Thine anger nor of those who go astray.

> *"When I err and go astray,*
> *You can help me find my way.*
> *When I work or poetize,*
> *Help the right direction rise."*

On page two, from Sura One,
Like a rising, guiding Sun,
Goethe in *West-East Divan*,
Wakes, then leads the reader on.

Goethe and Muhammad pray
To their God to grant that they
May be favored with a right
Knowledge of the path of light.

From the East and from the West
Goethe and the Prophet best
Know that Allah's solar fire
Symbolizes mind-desire.

77.

Lyrical Response to Verses from Sura 2
"The Cow" and Rumi-Thoughts in Schimmel

30. And when thy Lord said unto the angels: Lo! I am about to place a viceroy in the earth, they said: Wilt Thou place therein one who will do harm therein and will shed blood, while we, we hymn Thy praise and sanctify Thee? He said: Surely I know that which ye know not.

. . . . .

138. (We take our) colour from Allah, and who is better than Allah at colouring. We are His worshippers.

Did not the angels cry out in horror when the Lord told them . . . that He would place a vice-regent on earth, whereupon they foresaw that the new creature would be "blood-shedding and ignorant" (Sura 2/30). But God knew better what He was planning. . . . (Annemarie Schimmel, Rumi's World: The Life and Work of the Great Sufi Poet [Boston: Shambhala, 2001], 90–1)

Yet Maulana . . . speaks of pieces of cloth that fall into the dyeing vat . . . and thereby experiencee . . . the "dyeing of God," in which all colors disappear and only the radiant white remains, whereupon they sing joyfully, "I am the vat." (Annemarie Schimmel, Rumi's World, 134)

> More scandalous in man than being made
> Of altered clay, to one of altar-fire
> Fashioned, and likelier to kindle ire:
> His bloodlust! Violence, if unallayed,
>
> Menaced the cosmic harmony entire!
> But Allah something knew, yet undisplayed.
> Dyed in the vat divine, and new-arrayed
> In brilliance — gone the crimson flaw — in choir
>
> The viceroys might, with angel-mind, aspire,
> Sing in a purity of high desire,
> As of the Prophet on the mountain. May
>
> We, too, be cleansed, fresh-hearted, in the way
> Muhammad, bearing sorrow, came to be
> Through ministrations of the angels three.

78.

Lyrical Response to a Verse from Sura 2 "The Cow" and a Goethe Quatrain

---

142. .... Say: Unto Allah belong the East and the West. He guideth whom He will unto a straight path.

"*To God belongs the Orient,*
To God belongs the Occident;
The Northern and the Southern lands
Resting, tranquil, in His hands."

Goethe wrote these dawning rhymes
In Napoleonic times.
North and South and West and East —
Brother-battles never ceased.

Fighting is a nightmare through
Which he lived and hoped to view
Peace: when will the morning break?
May we from our mourning wake?

Selfhood sharpens enmity
In resentment, so that we
With our foes, hard heart the same,
Look like Hate, and take its name.

Would you learn to treasure free
Individuality?
Sibling-form before you place:
View the soul within the face.

Love the ray within the eyes
That their light to Height allies:
Bright concentric spheric skies
As when sun through heaven hies.

Love, that travels high and far,
Came to make us what we are.
Shed the veil, with ashes mixed:
Loose the serpent sting infixed.

Cast away what will distort
And a-borning life abort.
Joy derive when in the eye
Of your lover you espy

Sky-delight yourself have made.
Arms protective, gentle shade
Of a shelter, helpful, make.
Given love the hue will take

Of the mirroring desire
Sung and hymned by solar fire
In the eyes of one you love
Whom the moon was dreaming of.

79.

Lyrical Response to a Verse from Sura 2 "The Cow" and Goethe Quatrains

142. The foolish of the people will say: What hath turned them from the qiblah [place toward which the worshiper is turned at prayer] *which they formerly observed? Say: Unto Allah belong the East and the West. He guideth whom He will unto a straight path.*

In the right direction turn:
Praying, pious rite observe.
And the wise will never swerve,
Pride to serve and light to spurn;

They've an understanding of
Allah's guiding primacy:
East and West let meet in love —
Friends, and freed of rivalry.

Pearl of grace, each Goethe word,
Faithful to Muhammad's mind;
What the Prophet, thoughtful, heard,
Wisely guided he divined:

"Who knows himself and others well
No longer may ignore:
Orient, Occident can dwell
Separately no more."

"To God belongs the Orient,
To God belongs the Occident.
The Northern and the Southern lands
Resting, tranquil, in His hands."

80.

Lyrical Response to a Verse from Sura 5
"The Table Spread" and a Line from Rumi

---

110. . . . Remember . . . how thou didst shape of clay as it were the likeness of a bird by My permission, and didst blow upon it and it was a bird by My permission. . . .

"As much as you blow into me, that much do I fly upwards." Rumi, quoted in Annemarie Schimmel, The Triumphal Sun, *181*

The animal whose patterned tones are as a breath-bouquet
With rich, aroma-dizzied wine given to someone near,
As unrequested as the air of life, pure, limpid, clear
Sound-water stirred with dawnlight ripples where wind-windings play —

What do I tell about? I name the nature of a bird.
Now ask me what a lover is, and I the same will say.
His spirit breathes on the beloved's heart, and then we hear
A life infused by what the breather hoped and wanted heard.

We next inquire: what is a rebec, flute of blue, tambour?
It's a beloved and a bird and bloom and wine. His word,
Lover-musician, is blood-uttered, like a sun-drenched spear
Of grass agleam in spirit-sweetness, fire-refined and pure.

Jesus' creation of a bird from clay is like the sure
Instilling of Elisha's life into the child who lay
Dead till the heat infusion spreading livened, worked, and spurred
The boy to rise who, seven times, sneezed and then walked away.

81.

Lyrical Response to Verses from Sura 6 "Cattle" and Goethe Quatrains

---

96. Lo! Allah (it is) who splitteth the grain of corn and the date-stone (for sprouting). He bringeth forth the living from the dead, and is the bringer-forth of the dead from the living. Such is Allah. . . .

97. He is the Cleaver of the Daybreak, and He hath appointed the night for stillness, and the sun and the moon for reckoning. That is the measuring of the Mighty, the Wise.

98. And He it is Who hath set for you the stars that ye may guide your course by them amid the darkness of the land and the sea.

Freethought

Let me get my saddle, don't need rest!
Stay in hut and tent, for you they're best!
I'll be riding footloose, free, and far;
And above my cap, many a star.

He set the stars, that you may guide
Your course, by land and sea;
That you may take delight, beside,
Looking up steadily.

    (J. W. von Goethe)

What is the measure of the Mighty, Wise?
To look as high as you are seeing far;
Above your cap, free traveler, the star.
Cleaver of Daybreak, in the stilly skies

He put the calm that can itself advise:
The journeyings the Destination are.
The mind will find what might the body bar.
The grain, the date-stone from the dead arise.

Liberty's own invention-urge implies
A will that when the startled eagle flies
Can activate the drive that in us lies

To cry before the dawning when one dies:
I am the light I seek, wave-reservoir
If all is Allah, and His avatar.

82.

Lyrical Response to a Verse from Sura 6 "Cattle" and Rumi-Thoughts in Schimmel

96. . . . He bringeth forth the living from the dead. . . .

The central point in Rumi's view about creation is that of a creatio ex nihilo *— God has produced everything from* 'adam, *"nothingness" or "non-existence." . . . Every leaf and every green tree in spring becomes, for Jalāloddin, a messenger from* 'adam, *for they point to God's power to create lovely things from nothingness. . . . The* 'adam *is the hidden ground which God has concealed under the veil of existence; it is the sea of which only the foam is visible, or the wind which can be perceived only through the movement of the stirred up dust. . . . The Koran has attested that God "brings forth life from death," (Sura 6/96 etc.) and that means, in more scholarly language, that He produces being from not-being. . . . The image of non-existence,* 'adam, *as a box, mine, or ocean could lead easily to the conclusion that creation consists in giving form to entities already existent at least in the Divine Knowledge. Rumi is not clear upon this point, but his whole approach shows rather the* 'adam *as an unfathomable depth of nothingness which is endowed with existence only so far as God speaks to it and looks at it. . . . (Annemarie Schimmel,* The Triumphal Sun, *239–41)*

The 'adam's more than half of Adam and of me:
Ocean of hope, whereof we merely see the foam;
The stirred-up-dust-enwhirling wind, our deeper home;
The nothing of Becoming, and the secret key

To feeling for the Time that is our breathing. Free
In vastitude of room, nepheliadic, roam!
What can unite the light of day, the night of loam?
The nil whence all have come, and whither enter we.

We can't exhale but into empty air — you see?
We can't bring in but wingèd wind. The heaven-dome,
Robin's-egg blue? But nothing's there! Vacuity,

Unsoundable and boundless, where eternally
The yearning of "I will" becomes a brief "to be,"
Splendid, quick-ending, El Dorado-catacomb.

83.

Lyrical Response to Verses from Sura 7 "The Heights" and Hallaj-Thoughts in Schimmel: Soliloquy of Satan

---

10. And We have given you (mankind) power in the earth, and appointed for you therein a livelihood. Little give ye thanks!

11. We created you, then fashioned you, then told the angels: Fall ye prostrate before Adam! And they fell prostrate, all save Iblîs, who was not of those who make prostration.

12. He said: What hindered thee that thou didst not fall prostrate when I bade thee? (Iblîs) said: I am better than he. Thou createdst me of fire while him Thou didst create of mud.

13. He said: Then go down hence! It is not for thee to show pride here, so go forth! Lo! thou art of those degraded.

My portrait is of Iblis (diabolos, Devil) as perceived from an unusual viewpoint by poet Hallaj. I learned of the perspective of Hallaj from the prose account of his thought by Annemarie Schimmel in her *Islam: An Introduction* (Albany, State University of New York Press, 1992), 84.

> "I could not like that creature made of clay —
> Ev'n were he formed of pure essential fire,
> As *I* am, and the other jinns! Away!
> Even if Adam answered my desire
>
> To see a being radiant in array,
> Glowing as red-gold pyrope fiery-eyed,
> How might I turn my godly oath aside
> To bow to mortal and to finite? May

I, who have loved wise Allah, be denied
Requital of that yearning upward ray?
To gaze at man, look down, and — face — the mire!

I cannot be Your foe. I am a lyre:
Upon my heartstrings winds of Allah play.
I don't love man, won't see him deified."

84.

Lyrical Response to Verses from Sura 7
"The Heights" and Rumi-Thoughts in Schimmel

40. *Lo! they who deny Our revelations and scorn them, for them the gates of Heaven will not be opened nor will they enter the Garden until the camel goeth through the needle's eye. . . .*

42. *But (as for) those who believe and do good works — We tax not any soul beyond its scope — such are the rightful owners of the Garden. They abide therein.*

Rumi alludes also several times to the evangelical-Koranic parable of the camel and the needle's eye (Sura 7/40): here, again, love is the camel which does not fit into the narrow hold of human intellect. . . . The soul-camel is described best in the touching verses which speak of the herdsman who takes the animals every night into the pastures of Non-Existence, where they graze on the greenery of Divine gifts, with their eyes bound so that they cannot recognize the Divine Path on which they walk when the body sleeps. (Annemarie Schimmel, The Triumphal Sun, *95)*

> The camel in the Jesus-tale, beset by wealth,
> Entered no greening Eden of a needle eye.
> Soul-Camel, tired in blindfold, goes unminding by
> The trees and rills of nil-emergent heaven-health.
>
> These — merely needy. But the camel of our Love?
> He cannot fit into the hold of intellect,
> Yet is he bold and holy, though in one respect
> Awkward — the body, baffled by the breath above.
>
> Yet God will burden not the soul beyond our scope.
> Simoom, sirocco seem to hide a scanty hope;
> Sweet Eden green ungranted, blind in mind, we grope;
>
> And yet a camel has, at last, capacity
> Unfaltering to plod, not overawed, as we
> The camel-Adams, battling our fatigue, may be.

85.

Lyrical Response to a Verse from Sura 7 "The Heights" and Rumi-Thoughts in Schimmel

143. And when Moses came to Our appointed tryst and his Lord had spoken unto him, he said: My Lord! Show me (Thy self), that I may gaze upon Thee. HE said: Thou wilt not see Me, but gaze upon the mountain! If it stand still in its place, then thou wilt see Me. And when his Lord revealed (His) glory to the mountain He sent it crashing down. And Moses fell down senseless. And when he woke he said: Glory unto Thee! I turn unto Thee repentant, and I am the first of (true) believers.

Every movement can be explained as dance — even the Koranic dictum that during God's relevation on Mount Sinai the mountain trembled (Sura 7/143) is interpreted as its entering into ecstatic dance, comparable to the perfect Sufi in the Divine Presence. Did not Abraham dance in the fire, and Jesus, and whoever partook in the spiritual pilgrimage? (Annemarie Schimmel, The Triumphal Sun, *220)*

> Moses had fainted when the mountain danced —
> Fell, and awakened, felt the glory there
> That trembled, rending, in the shaken air
> Whereon shaft-lightning of the Lord had glanced.
>
> The hills had skipped for David, who enhanced,
> Thankful, before the ark, a heartfelt prayer
> Dancing, as Abraham, who his betrayer
> Forgave as flames were cooled when they advanced.
>
> I see the holy three within the flame
> Dancing when suddenly the fourth one came
> To join, angelic, in the white-hot glow:
>
> Shadrach and Meshach and Abed-nego
> And their divine companion whirl and turn —
> With yearning love alone their blood will burn.

86.

Lyrical Response to Verses from Sura 7 "The Heights" and Sura 42 "Counsel" and Rumi-Thoughts in Schimmel

-----

7:172. And (remember) when thy Lord brought forth from the Children of Adam, from their reins, their seed, and made them testify of themselves, (saying): Am I not your Lord? They said: Yea, verily. We testify. (That was) lest ye should say at the Day of Resurrection: Lo! of this we were unaware. . . .

42:43. And verily whoso is patient and forgiveth — lo! that, verily, is (of) the stedfast heart of things.

The dance of the rivers and trees is a repetition of that dance performed on the day of the Primordial Covenant, when God addressed not-yet-created humanity with His word: . . . "Am I not your Lord? (Sura 7/172). Rumi understands this divine address as music that made all creatures come forth in a happy dance. . . . (Annemarie Schimmel, Rumi's World, 61)

Images related to the realm of fire are always connected with suffering. . . . But the Sufis had invented a fine pun: when . . . the not-yet-created humanity responded to God's question A-lastu bi-rabbikum, "Am I not your Lord?," with the word bala, "Yes, certainly" (Sura 7/172), people accepted all the affliction, balā, that was to visit them in His service. . . . (Rumi's World, 178)

A Covenant Primordial was made
Before the race of Adam came to be.
The pre-world soul-seeds in Eternity
Uttered assent in faith which would not fade.

Then did they dance, in radiance arrayed
Mid this, their pre-creation revelry?
Or were they saddened by affliction, fee
That must by every mortal yet be paid?

I love the Rumi double focus. Both
Were felt, and are today. Let none be loth
To dance, and to withstand the moral test.

Those who were beggars are the better kings.
To learn of low and high in life were best.
Patience and pardon — at the heart of things.

87.

Lyrical Response to Verses from Sura 8
"The Spoils of War" and Sura 25 "The Criterion"
and Rumi-Thoughts in Schimmel

8:17. . . . And thou (Muhammad) threwest not when thou didst throw, but Allah threw, that He might test the believers by a fair test from Him. Lo! Allah is Hearer, Knower.

25:51. If We willed, We could raise up a warner in every village.

. . . Shams said that "God Himself cannot do without Muhammad. . . ." It is Muhammad "in whom the whole world will get lost," as his nurse Halima was told when she was worried because the child had been lost. . . . Hence Maulana's . . . allusions to . . . the verse "You did not cast when you cast" (Sura 8/17), affirming that the Prophet was the instrument through which God worked. (Annemarie Schimmel, Rumi's World, *124)*

> *Thou threwest not when thou didst throw, but Allah threw.*
> He chose Muhammad as a mirror, wherein lost
> All might be found, the self cast off, proud imp well tossed.
> There is a race that none may run so well as you.
>
> *Thou threwest not when thou didst throw, but Allah threw.*
> Everyone has a place, no pointless duplication,
> For it would vitiate the joy of the Creation.
> There is a race that none may run so well as you.
>
> *Thou threwest not when thou didst throw, but Allah threw.*
> Shams, friend of Rumi, had a name that meant the Sun.
> You are emblazoned with the same, no less a one.
> There is a race that none may run so well as you.
>
> *Thou threwest not when thou didst throw, but Allah threw.*
> In image of the Lord of Heaven generated,
> Boldly go fated forth in solar force elated.
> There is a race that none may run so well as you.

Thou threwest not when thou didst throw, but Allah threw.
God could not do without Muhammad, for his goal
Would aid in radiant way the saving of the Soul.
There is a race that none may run so well as you.

Thou threwest not when thou didst throw, but Allah threw.
Who but Mevlana, made to play the wailing flute,
Could thrill the rose-tree spirit so, from bloom to root?
There is a race that none may run so well as you.

88.

Lyrical Response to Verses from Sura 9 "Repentance" and Rumi's Words in Schimmel

111. Lo! Allah hath bought from the believers their lives and their wealth because the Garden will be theirs; they shall fight in the way of Allah and shall slay and be slain. It is a promise which is binding on Him in the Torah and the Gospel and the Qur'an. Who fulfilleth His convenant better than Allah? Rejoice then in your bargain that ye have made, for that is the supreme triumph.

112. (Triumphant) are those who turn in repentance (to Allah), those who serve (Him), those who praise (Him), those who fast, those who bow down, those who fall prostrate (in worship), those who enjoin the right and who forbid the wrong and those who keep the limits (ordained) of Allah — And give glad tidings to believers!

Maulana . . . applies the Koranic saying "God will buy your souls" (Sura 9/111) to the transformation of ice into water. He will buy ice (a substance used . . . to cool sherbets . . .) from . . . human beings and give them in exchange "a sweet melting". . . . Then . . . the army of rose gardens and fragrant herbs reigns victorious, the lilies have sharpened their swords and daggers. . . . (Annemarie Schimmel, Rumi's World, *53–54)*

> When Allah buys the winter sherbet-ice wherewith
> We had been well supplied, behold! in glorious war
> Displayed, the lordly moral souls were waiting for:
> Sword of the lily, dagger-thorn of rose — the pith
>
> And gist of life below can pierce what froze above!
> Triumphant they who bow, fall prostrate, fast, and praise,
> Abasing *nafs*, the matter-self, whose bounded ways,
> Blast the releasing root that would bloom up in love.
>
> A winter-prison open, springtime souls are free.
> Aromas rule within the fragrant herbal garden.
> We feel redeemed, bought back through Allah's godly pardon.
>
> Torah and Gospel and Qur'an in this agree:
> A rising fire had conquered what was cold, hibernal.
> Blind ego dies. The world is warmed in Soul Eternal.

89.

Lyrical Response to Verses from Sura 12 "Joseph" and Rumi-Thoughts in Schimmel

---

16. And they came weeping to their father in the evening.

17. Saying: O our father! We went racing one with another, and left Joseph by our things, and the wolf devoured him, and thou believest not our saying even when we speak the truth.

18. And they came with false blood on his shirt. He said: Nay, but your minds have beguiled you into something. (My course is) comely patience. And Allah it is whose help is to be sought in that (predicament) which ye describe. [...]

91. Go with this shirt of mine and lay it on my father's face, he will become (again) a seer; and come to me with all your folk.

94. When the caravan departed their father had said: Truly I am conscious of the breath of Joseph, though ye call me dotard.

95. (Those around him) said: By Allah, lo! thou art in thine old aberration.

96. Then, when the bearer of glad tidings came, he laid it on his face and he became a seer once more. He said: Said I not unto you that I know from Allah that which ye know not?

... winter can ... be seen as the season of "gathering for the sake of spending." [...] Thus everyone ... has to practice "fine patience" (Sura 12/18) throughout ... winter..., following the example of the trees, which, like blind Jacob, wait patiently for the day when the spring's fragrant breeze will bring them "the scent of Yusuf's shirt," the aroma of the first buds.... And the trees' patience is required ... to collect the sap in the roots and to spend it ... when the sun caresses the twigs. (Annemarie Schimmel, Rumi's World, *54)*

> Agèd, he'd gathered for the spending. He
> Had never been so blinded and bereft
> Of prophet-art that nothing would be left.
> He'd known the brothers lied. For like a tree
>
> Awaiting airy angeling to free
> Aroma from the soul of soil that slept
> Was Jacob. Flame-seed in the spirit leapt.
> What could the Joseph-jailers know? Ah me!

Blest be the vernal messenger. Amen.
The mercy-shirt upon the father-face
Averred the verity of godly grace.

Dormant the force in chilly winter when
The streams of Eden lie in ice — Arise!
Nard, aloe, cardamom voice hearty cries.

90.

Lyrical Response to a Verse from Sura 12 "Joseph" and Thoughts in Schimmel's Islam

53. I do not exculpate myself. Lo! the (human) soul enjoineth unto evil, save that whereon my Lord has mercy. Lo! my Lord is Forgiving, Merciful.

"... *the first-known ascetics of the Iraqi and Syrian lands ... constantly fought against the* nafs, *the lower soul principle that 'instigates to evil' (Sura 12/53)....*" Annemarie Schimmel, Islam: An Introduction, *104*

"'*The* nafs *has a Koran and a rosary in the one hand and a dagger in the sleeve.'*" Schimmel, Islam, *104*

"*The poor, however, who is grateful — even for not receiving anything — is superior to all others, for gratitude, like all other stations on the mystical path, has three stages: thanks for receiving something, thanks for not receiving it, and gratitude for the capacity of being grateful.*" Schimmel, Islam, *103*

Koran and rosary in hand, a dagger in the sleeve:
Ninety-nine names of God on beads — barely will these avail.
The lower hides to catch the higher qualities, which quail.
Yet "All is Allah," claim wise later seekers who believe.

Koran and rosary in hand, a dagger in the sleeve:
That is the *nafs*, a clay encasing. Yet the flame won't fail:
Tormented wild by portents, it will strive and writhe and flail.
There is a light that loves the Sun and has the pow'r to shrieve.

I'm thankful for my being thankful. Gratitude's a grace.
To love your neighbor *as* and *and* yourself will keep in place
The stable center of the gyroscope of whirling joy.

Faqrí fakhrí — "My poverty's my pride," the Prophet said.
"Ah(m)ad," he knew *ahad*, pure Unity! — with no allòy,
No lower *nafs* — and all recalled resentments quieted.

91.

Lyrical Response to Verses from Sura 15 "Al Ḥijr" and Sura 33 "The Clans" and Rumi-Thoughts in Schimmel

---

15:29. So, when I have made him and breathed into him of My spirit, do ye fall down, prostrating yourselves unto him.

33:72. Lo! We offered the trust unto the heavens and the earth and hills, but they shrank from bearing it and were afraid of it. And man assumed it. Lo! he hath proved a tyrant and a fool.

... the Divine amāna, *the "entrusted good," is the most important and ... most endangered element in human beings.... For Rumi the* amāna *is the gift of responsibility, of free choice, of a human being's ability to recognize the spiritual aspects of his being and develop them. (Annemarie Schimmel,* Rumi's World, *92)*

> The mountains and the heaven and the earth decline
> The present of *amāna*, lightsome yoke of Trust.
> The acorn loves becoming oak. What burden? Must
> A heavy lethargy have darkened the divine?
>
> Yes. A perplexing leaven then like Eden-wine
> Entered the head of Adam. Sundered from the dust,
> He felt a levity that exiled lower lust:
> Freedom to make himself each day a life-design.
>
> Mind-moving wind of Spirit spread *amāna* vast.
> Adam-Imaginer might future all the past:
> The calling palm would tell him "Tall!," the earth confirm
>
> A steadiness of tread, blooms gentle him, the worm
> And cloud put down, raise high, the jinn bestir, the gem
> Burnish the facets. He would name himself and them.

92.

Lyrical Response to a Verse from Sura 17
"The Children of Israel"
and Rumi-Thoughts in Schimmel

In the name of Allah, the Beneficent, the Merciful.

1. Glorified be He Who carried His servant by night from the Inviolable Place of Worship to the Far Distant Place of wortship the neighbourhood whereof We have blessed, that We might show him of Our tokens! Lo! He, only He, is the Hearer, the Seer.

This Divine Love manifested itself best in the experience of the isrā, *the Night-Journey, the ascension to heaven to which the Koran (Sura 17/1) alludes: "Praised be He who travelled with His servant at night". . . . The Prophet who "dedicated his day to work and gain, and his night to (Divine) love," because his "heart was awake even though his eyes slept," as the* hadith *says, was uplifted on the miraculous steed,* Borāq, *whose very name became among the mystics and particularly with Rumi equivalent to "love." . . . according to tradition, Gabriel, the guide of the heavenly journey, remained outside the Divine Presence into which the Prophet was admitted; for even the angel of inspiration "did not dare to fly further lest his wings be singed"; thus he becomes the symbol of reason which cannot transgress a certain point. (Schimmel,* The Triumphal Sun, *285)*

> Buraq is Love, that Reason had to leave behind,
> For he is light, not heat, and so, lest wing be singed,
> Farther from Allah stayed. No pride of mind impinged...
> Yet would not full awareness needed be to find
>
> One's place and meaning in the Presence? Could the blind
> Leader (if reasonless), a horse however swift,
> Without the amply active Intellect yet lift
> A viewless eye toward the source of humankind?

No, Love and Reason will combine in my Buraq!
Joined in Imagination, they will go to God and back,
Aye, both at once, as with a double-pointed lance.

Borne by the holy force of lordly metaphor,
Bearer-Beyond, are Gabriel and horse and more
One with the might of eye in Allah's lightning glance.

93.

Lyrical Response to Verses from Sura 19 "Mary" and a Comment in Schimmel's Rumi

---

23. And the pangs of childbirth drove her unto the trunk of the palm-tree. She said: Oh, would that I had died ere this and had become a thing of naught, forgotten!

24. Then (one) cried unto her from below her, saying: Grieve not! Thy Lord hath placed a rivulet beneath thee,

25. And shake the trunk of the palm-tree toward thee, thou wilt cause ripe dates to fall upon thee.

26. So eat and drink and be consoled. . . .

The body is like Mary. Each of us has a Jesus, but so long as no pain appears, our Jesus is not born. If pain never comes, our Jesus goes back to his place of origin on the same secret path he had come, and we remain . . . without a share of him. (Rumi, qtd. in Annemarie Schimmel, *Rumi's World*, 122)

> The Jesus of our body's born from pain,
> So Rumi tells. Yet water, palm-tree, dates
> Nourish the sufferer, who celebrates
> What she could never otherwise attain.
>
> Such trial is the guide to godly gain:
> Dark mind is driven hard to bear a soul;
> Heart will be riven, that it may be whole.
> From thorn to Jordan, fear to Eden-plain.
>
> The sorrow-journey is both road and goal,
> Wiser the traveler than those who wait:
> Prefer the path to fair and fine estate.
>
> To bear a rarer Jesus be your role:
> The dates, the rivulet, the favored rain
> From shaken palm-tree shall the child unchain.

94.

Lyrical Response to Verses from Sura 20 "Tâ Hâ" and Sura 28 "The Story" and Rumi-Thoughts from Schimmel; FitzGerald/Omar

20:22. And thrust thy hand within thine armpit, it will come forth white without hurt. . . .

28:32. Thrust thy hand into the bosom of thy robe, it will come forth white without hurt. . . .

The lily praises the beauty of the rose "with a hundred tongues" or manifests the miracle of the White Hand (Sura 20/22 et al.), by which Moses proved his prophetic status. (Annemarie Schimmel, Rumi's World, *63)*

Now the New Year reviving old Desires,
The thoughtful Soul to Solitude retires,
*   Where the White Hand of Moses on the bough*
Puts out, and Jesus from the Ground suspires.
    The Rubáiyát of Omar Khayyám, *tr. Edward FitzGerald*

> Where the white hand of Moses on the bough
> Appears, the virgin lily, vernal, sings
> And with more pure and paler beauty flings
> Rays only prophet-praising will allow.
>
> Where the white hand of Moses from within
> The garment had emerged it showed a white
> And all-including spirit-worldly light,
> Believers in their wandering to win.
>
> Where the white hand of Moses made a sign,
> Angelic joy, a gentle messenger,
> Gave the direction pious minds prefer:
> To them is lent the godly Garden wine.
>
> See the white hand of Moses, high above
> The people, pointing to the Promised Land,
> Brighter in hope than Noah-rainbow! Stand
> In awe before the journey-guiding Dove.

95.

Lyrical Response to Verses from Sura 21 "The Prophets" and Rumi-Thoughts in Schimmel

51. And We verily gave Abraham of old his proper course, and We were Aware of him. . . .

54. He said: Verily ye and your fathers were in plain error. . . .

57. And, by Allah, I shall circumvent your idols after ye have gone away and turned your backs.

58. Then he reduced them to fragments, all save the chief of them, that haply they might have recourse to it.

59. They said: Who hath done this to our gods? Surely it must be some evil-doer. . . .

62. They said: Is it thou who hast done this to our gods, O Abraham?

63. He said: But this, their chief hath done it. So question them, if they can speak. . . .

65. And they were utterly confounded, and they said: Well thou knowest that these speak not. . . .

68. They cried: Burn him and stand by your gods, if ye will be doing.

69. We said: O fire, be coolness and peace for Abraham.

This living flame of Love inspires him, and like the sun this flame can burn away everything. . . . Yet Maulana enjoys the fire — for his soul . . . cannot live outside the fire. Just as in the Koranic story of Ibrahim (Sura 21/69), this fire becomes "cool and pleasant" to the lover. . . . (Annemarie Schimmel, Rumi's World, *177)*

> Abraham, sage, impatient man, idoloclast,
> By Allah's will found fire a coolness and a peace.
> How does the burning Rumi find such kind release?
> Can love alone provide the spirit rich repast?
>
> A lively sense of humor gently mild will aid
> In tempering the flame and turning it to rose.
> Relish the clever game, the ruse that soon of those
> Who Allah might defy a mockery had made.

A single thought may quell a million fiery jinns.
Fine wit will further what the riving light begins
And cast away with laughter madness from the soul.

More humor is more room. The roomier the mind
The mightier. Nasreddin Hodja, too, could find
A joke a gift — a yoke would lift — behold him whole.

96.

Lyrical Response to a Verse from Sura 21 "The Prophets" and Rumi-Thoughts in Schimmel

107. We sent thee not save as a mercy for the peoples.

The "rain of mercy" is . . . connected with the Prophet: . . . villagers in Anatolia . . . call rain . . . "mercy," and the relation between this . . . and the Prophet, . . . sent as "mercy for the worlds" . . . (Sura 21/107), is often intended when rain clouds appear in Maulana's poetry. (Annemarie Schimmel, Rumi's World, *59)*

*Muhammad is also described as visiting the sick . . . , and his kindness is like rain, for he was sent as "mercy for the worlds" (Sura 21/107). (*Rumi's World, *128)*

A rain of mercy for the waiting worlds, a way
To marry as with dew the earth and cooling sky
And split the hardness in the heart which with a cry
Of gratitude is riven that a fountain may

Arise of kindness for the blest created things
Wherein the pulsing elements their might combine:
The ardent blood in carmine fire, the hyaline
Light of the eye, the bones, the trees in widened rings,

Confirm the resting strength of soul-solidity,
The flesh that is of clay but yet can strive and sing —
All say their nature in the rain of prophecy,

The word of mercy for the world, acclaimed in me
And you and moving trees of Eden and the sea,
The waves that laughing clap their hands and hail the King.

97.

Lyrical Response to a Verse from Sura 22 "The Pilgrimage" and a Goethe Translation

15. Whoso is wont to think (through envy) that Allah will not give him (Muhammad) victory in the world and the Hereafter (and is enraged at the thought of his victory), let him stretch a rope up to the roof (of his dwelling), and let him hang himself. Then let him see whether his strategy dispelleth that whereat he rageth.

"One who's peeved that Allah's gleam
Grants Muhammad help and hope,
Let him fasten to a beam
In his hall a sturdy rope
And be hanged with knot well-tied.
He will feel that wrath subside."

So the poet Goethe wrote
In "The Prophet." Gracefully
He rephrases, and we note
Wide applicability.
It's a clever way to tell
Enemies to go to hell.

Isn't Allah, though, well-known
As benignant, merciful?
Has the writing wrathful grown?
Does it madden, anger's pull?
I would answer: humor goes
Quite a way to quell our woes.

Clever quips and wit dispel
Clouds of gloomy brooding wrath.
Wars and worries warrant well
That we tread a lighter path.
Sun smiles on the righteous — we
Laugh, replying readily.

98.

Lyrical Response to a Verse from Sura 22 "The Pilgrimage" and Verses by Blake

---

73. O mankind! A similitude is coined, so pay ye heed to it: Lo! those on whom ye call beside Allah will never create a fly though they combine together for the purpose. And if the fly took something from them, they could not rescue it from him. So weak are (both) the seeker and the sought!

Seest thou the little winged fly, smaller than a grain of sand?
It has a heart like thee; a brain open to heaven & hell,
Withinside wondrous & expansive; its gates are not clos'd,
I hope thine are not: hence it clothes itself in rich array;
Hence thou art cloth'd with human beauty O thou mortal man.
Seek not thy heavenly father then beyond the skies. . . .

—*William Blake,* Milton *20:27–32 (The Complete Poetry & Prose of William Blake, newly rev. ed. by David V. Erdman, Commentary by Harold Bloom [New York: Doubleday, 1988])*

> They err who underestimate
> The holiness of lowly state.
> A hero sought Olympus' top
> Whom yet a humble fly might stop.
> Such was the fate Bellerophon
> Beset. He had embarked upon
> A flight to meet his highest gods,
> Yet failed when fighting higher odds.
> For Pegasus, when fly-bit, fell,
> Unlike Buraq — not guided well.
>
> The humble fly appears to me
> The emblem of a prophecy:
> Their complicated compound eyes
> Thousands of lenses each comprise.
> The littlest movement they discern
> To which fine hearing makes them turn.
> Their minds attuned to hell and heaven

Are for our thought a lightsome leaven.
How sad the slander that denies
And Satan names the Lord of Flies!

With myriad optic open gates
The fly to heaven levitates!
Bright angels, they, of death and life,
Embodying the love and strife
That are the laws of nature here
Which may embitter or endear
But need be well attended to
By those with comprehending view.
Breathe in, then out: be stress, relief,
The twofold root of true belief.

99.

Lyrical Response to a Verse from Sura 28 "The Story," Rumi-Thoughts in Schimmel, and Goethe Quatrains

---

88. And cry not unto any other god along with Allah. There is no God save Him. Everything will perish save His countenance. . . .

. . . . .

Jalāloddin Rumi speaks:
> *You'd linger in the world — it, dreamlike, flees.*
> *Travel — but fate will say what land one sees.*
> *You can't hold back the heat, or keep the cold.*
> *And all that blooms will rapidly get old.*

Zuleika speaks:
> *In mirrors, beautiful am I.*
> *But fate will make me age, you say.*
> *Unchanging, we, in Allah's eye:*
> *Love Him in me — right now. Today.*

> *(J. W. von Goethe)*

The human 'I' has to be eliminated in God's presence. Rumi has illustrated this point in a tender story of a lover who, after maturing on a long journey, was admitted by the beloved; for after having lost his identity he answered the friend's question "Who is there?" saying "It is you!" . . . "Who is there?" cried his friend. He answered, "Thou, O charmer of all hearts!" "Now," said the friend, "since thou art I, come in: there is no room for two 'I's in this house." (Annemarie Schimmel, The Triumphal Sun, *309)*

As far as one can understand from scattered remarks . . . he firmly believed in the Ash'arite doctrine of constant re-creation: "God most High creates a man anew every moment, sending something perfectly fresh into his inner heart." (Schimmel, 263)

> Zuleika — downcast? Why, O Rumi wise?
> True, all the world will die, save Allah's face.
> Yet other countenances have their place,
> And in this moment. Why not love two I's?

Myriad mirrors let the mind surmise
The multiplicity of godly grace.
We'll gamely move in tune with time. Let race
The raving wind enlivened in the skies!

Moments engender, each, though speeding on,
The angel-flame of the Creation Dawn.
The life that I respire may soon be gone

Yet is a mirror of all minds that are
Kindled in vision by the Allah-star,
Faithful, reflecting on a Fire afar.

100.

Lyrical Response to a Verse from Sura 29 "The Spider," Rumi-Thoughts in Schimmel; Blake, Goethe Verses

---

41. The likeness of those who choose other patrons than Allah is as the likeness of the spider when she taketh unto herself a house, and lo! the frailest of all houses is the spider's house, if they but knew.

The spider resembles the selfish person who does not know anything besides enjoying and boasting of his own art, without attributing the true art to God. Lust, which spins veils before the soul, is again a spider, and in one of his finest verses Rumi compares the soul which weaves a net from its own thoughts and plans to the spider whose house, woven from its saliva ("the weakest of all houses," Sura 29/41), is soon destroyed, whereas the fabric God weaves by His plans, remains in eternity. (Annemarie Schimmel, The Triumphal Sun, *110)*

The wanton Boy that kills the Fly
Shall feel the spiders Enmity

    (William Blake, "Auguries of Innocence" ll. 33–34)

When a spider once I killed,
I was thoughtful: was it right?
To partake of day's delight
We'd been meant, as God had willed.

    (J. W. von Goethe, "Als ich einmal eine Spinne erschlagen")

> The silken thread, strong protein strand,
> Can trap a fly, in climbing aid,
> Or smooth a burrow wall once made,
> Hold sperm awhile, make egg sacs, and
>
> Do other kind or killing tasks.
> Lustful? Or selfish? Violent?
> The spider, on survival bent,
> Will answer as occasion asks.

When morning-hued in rainbow-guise,
Dewed web is radiant as eyes
(The thousand-lensed) of preyed-on flies.

Venom-injectors' jeweled jail,
Of all the houses made most frail,
May work full well before it fail.

101.

Lyrical Response to Sura 30 "The Romans" and Sura 31 "Luqmân"; Goethe Quatrain

---

30:46. . . . He sendeth herald winds to make you taste His mercy, and that the ships may sail at His command, and that ye may seek His favour, and that haply ye may be thankful. . . .

47. Allah is He who sendeth the winds so that they raise clouds, and spreadeth them along the sky as pleaseth Him, and causeth them to break and thou seest the rain downpouring from within them. And when He maketh it to fall on whom He will of His bondmen, lo! they rejoice. . . .

31:18. Turn not thy cheek in scorn toward folk, nor walk with pertness in the land. Lo! Allah loveth not each braggart boaster.

19. Be modest in thy bearing and subdue thy voice. . . .

31. Hast thou not seen how the ships glide on the sea by Allah's grace, that he may show you of His wonders? . . .

32. And if a wave enshroudeth them like awnings, they cry unto Allah. . . . But when He bringeth them safe to land, some of them compromise. None denieth Our signs save every traitor ingrate.

"How startling: what a marvel-feat,
With ugly Luqmân's aid!"
The cane-reed never will be sweet
Until the sugar's made.

   (J. W. von Goethe, "Was brachte Lokman nicht hervor")

> The herald wind He sends to make
> You taste great mercy; that the ships
> May sail at His command, and so
> You may His favor, thankful, seek.

The gliding ship He may not shake
But by His grace it lifts and dips.
Should waves like awning-shroudings go
Amok, swift words of calm He'll speak.

Cloud-raising winds, before they break
In rain to wet the heat-cracked lips
Of whom He will, float spreading, grow
To please not froward folk, but meek.

The braggart boaster must awake
Who when the furious thunder rips
Gains aid, but later, sullen foe,
Proves, traitor ingrate, faithless, weak.

Walkers with pertness cannot slake
A thirsty pride. Their whimsy whips
The tearful wind in willful woe
As blamable as it is bleak.

Like to a tranquil, dawning lake
Whose balanced lull no rowboat tips,
Be modest and to anger slow:
Turn not in scorn a haughty cheek.

102.

Lyrical Response to Verses from Sura 31 "Luqmân" and Sura 62 "The Congregation" and Rumi-Thoughts in Schimmel: An Imaginary Dialogue

31:19. Be modest in thy bearing and subdue thy voice. Lo! the harshest of all voices is the voice of the ass.

62:5. The likeness of those who are entrusted with the Law of Moses, yet apply it not, is as the likeness of the ass carrying books. . . .

Perhaps Maulana saw all this with his inner eye as he strolled through the springtime gardens of Konya and observed the chirping birds, the lively rabbits and cunning foxes, and listened with disgust to the donkeys whose braying the Koran calls "the ugliest voice" (Sura 31/19). Typical creature of the world of matter, sensual and delighting in filth — how could a donkey enjoy spiritual beauty or feel the refreshing breeze that comes like the breath of Jesus? No, Maulana did not care if a donkey got lost; in fact, one should be happy to be rid of such an animal! (Annemarie Schimmel, Rumi's World, *69)*

Love defies any intellectual task of explanation. Intellect is indeed "like the donkey that carries books" (Sura 62/5), as the mystics, and among them Rumi, have often repeated with the Koranic expression. It is a lame donkey, not comparable to the winged Borāq, which carried Mohammad into the divine Presence. (Annemarie Schimmel, The Triumphal Sun, *336)*

> Mevlana Rumi on the road
> Met Hodja with a heavy load
> On donkey-back, the raucous bray
> Audible many miles away!
>
> The martyr-donkey marketward
> Bore burdens purchasers preferred:
> Cardamom, aloe, basil, nard;
> Mangoes and melons meet, unmarred.

"I so have loathed th'unholy sound,"
Rumi proclaimed, "that floats around
The lowness of the loam-born brain
Flailing in failure's old refrain!

From filth and sensuality
And ills no friend may ever free
That form by the refreshing breeze
Of Jesus' breath in Eden ease.

The beast at best is Intellect,
Which, vainly claiming to 'reflect,'
Mirrors no guide but mortal pride
And so must in the dust abide.

Outdistanced by abounding Love,
It will not seek the spheres above,
Where never-lamed, the famed Buraq
Had brought the Prophet on his back."

Said Hodja: "Labor and delay
And wayward rains the plaguy way
Will greatly lengthen for the one
Whom burdens bend in summer sun.

For though it be no Rumi-flute,
The bray is heralding the fruit
Of effort-needing hero-work
That sweat-drenched Adam shouldn't shirk.

Descending from the firmament,
Would your Buraq be well content
To carry, at his daily task,
Heavily laden, all we ask?

Two Tables of the Law I see,
Called Love and Labor. Willingly
The Spirit shall the Body move
To lift the heart in works of love

Ever allied with life of Mind,
Which can the grand devices find
Enabling Woman, Child, and Man
To plan, and carry out the plan."

Instilled with this exalted laud
(For "Hodja" means a "man of God"),
Great joys in donkey-brays assault
The ears of jinns in heaven-vault.

And lo! the horse of Rumi's heard
Choiring along with equine word:
The praises of the sage he neighs,
Joining his voice with donkey-brays.

103.

Lyrical Response to Verses from Sura 37
"Those Who Set the Ranks,"
Verses of Goethe, Omar/FitzGerald

42. . . . And they will be honoured

43. In the Gardens of delight,

44. On couches facing one another;

45. A cup from a gushing spring is brought round for them,

46. White, delicious to the drinkers,

47. Wherein there is no headache nor are they made mad thereby,

48. And with them are those of modest gaze, with lovely eyes,

49. (Pure) as they were hidden eggs (of the ostrich).

You're always safe, I'd say —
To you, the best belongs:
Two friends, all cares away;
Wine goblet, book of songs.

    (J. W. von Goethe, "Du bist auf immer geborgen")

A Book of Verses underneath the Bough,
A Loaf of Bread, a Jug of Wine — and Thou
Beside me singing in the Wilderness —
Ah! Wilderness were Paradise enow.

(The Rubáiyát of Omar Khayyám, *tr. Edward FitzGerald*, XII)

      The Allah-coined similitudes
      Convey in metaphoric moods
      Gifts, to the righteous and the wise,
      Constitutive of Paradise.

      Omar and Goethe join to say
      That Eden-wine and poems may
      As two fine friends regarded be.
      Kòran and Omar offer three.

With lovely eyes and modest gaze
The third companion lends our days
In Eden kindly company,
Shy and defined by purity.

The scripture does not claim she sings.
Yet that would be the treat of kings,
Melding the wine and poetry
In melismatic melody.

The houri-music ears would bless
Turning a meager wilderness
Into the highest wine-allure,
Paradisiacal and pure.

104.

Lyrical Response to a Verse from Sura 51
"The Winnowing Winds" and
Rumi-Thoughts in Schimmel

---

56. I created the jinn and humankind only that they might worship Me.

Everything has to attest God's Greatness; evil and good, suffering and joy are nothing but instruments to lead man towards his duty and to the goal of his life which is permanent adoration of God as it is said in the Koran: "Verily We created spirits and men that they might worship" (Sura 51/56).

That is why Rumi praises God's power in ever new verses.... Take the lovely words in the story of the poor Sufi:

He who turns the fire into roses and trees is also able to make this (world fire) harmless. (Annemarie Schimmel, The Triumphal Sun, 235)

Rumi's main topic is ... the dance of the zarrāt, *the tiny dust particles which are seen moving in the sunlight; the word* zarra *can also be translated as 'atom' which gives this imagery a very modern, but appropriate flavour. These particles are thought to dance around the sun; the Sun of Tabriz is the centre around which everything turns.... It is out of love for this sun that the atoms of this world came dancing forth from Non-Existence. (Schimmel, 220)*

> The fire of jinn and of the heated blood and kind,
> And of the tree and rose, of lightning and the star,
> And of the shining *zarra*-energies that are
> The meaning of the life that cries within the mind
>
> In dervish-whirl enrobed, hot-white in pious wise,
> The fierce devotion of the flame that, in the tears
> Of solar-system iris-wide concentered spheres,
> Will pour with rainbow brightness burning love that sighs

Tells of an elder depth of gratitude than I
Could ever be aware of, till from out the cry
Of happiness alive a chant that can but weep

In hymn fulfills the air, like to a mighty bell
While atoms in my heart and hands will clap and leap
And lordly-ordered carmine orbit-ardor keep.

105.

Lyrical Response to Verses from Sura 87 "The Most High" and Sura 103 "The Declining Day," Ecclesiastes, Micah

---

87:1. Praise the name of thy Lord the Most High,

2. Who createth, then disposeth;

3. Who measureth, then guideth;

4. Who bringeth forth the pasturage,

5. Then turneth it to russet stubble.

103. In the name of Allah, the Beneficent, the Merciful.

1. By the declining day,

2. Lo! man is in a state of loss,

3. Save those who believe and do good works, and exhort one another to truth and exhort one another to endurance.

Let us hear the conclusion of the whole matter: fear God, and keep his commandments: for this is the whole duty of man.

   (Ecclesiastes [Koheleth] 12:13)

He hath shewed thee, O man, what is good; and what doth the Lord require of thee, but to do justly, and to love mercy, and to walk humbly with thy God?

   (Micah 6:8)

In circlings of the world, when life is turned
To death, and pasture — leveled russet stubble;
Emblemed, the tomb, in every hump and nubble;
Ember, the fading fire that early burned;

Reft is the bird that in pearl-heaven perned;
Empty the sky of all but coming trouble;
Gone from the spring — glint, purling wave, and bubble;
Yester the year when youth for world-wealth yearned;

What can we do in our declining day?
Season in sky and field requires that we
Abide with duty and by work endure.

Justice and mercy and humility
In faithful daily labor will assure
Our living merge with nature's braver way.

106.

Lyrical Response to Verses from Sura 89 "The Dawn" and to Rumi and Other Sufi Thoughts in Schimmel

27. But ah! thou soul at peace!

28. Return unto the Lord, content in His good pleasure!

... the falcon ... becomes a symbol of the "soul at peace" (Sura 89/27) ... called home by its Creator, and ... Maulana shows us the proud bird ... asking forgiveness for his trespasses. ... (Annemarie Schimmel, Rumi's World, *68)*

A story from the tenth century tells that a Sufi addressed God in his prayer:

"O Lord, are you satisfied with me that I am satisfied with You?"

He heard a voice: "You liar! if you were satisfied with Me you would not ask whether I am satisfied with you!" (Annemarie Schimmel, Islam: An Introduction, *104)*

Maulana's falcon-friend, on climbing to the height,
Asks if the Lord with him is truly satisfied,
All sin forgiving. Yet, though manifest the pride,
I do not view a soul at peace in Master-light.

Petitionary praying? Hesitant, or tense;
Supreme tranquillity, calm-confident and brave.
Humble desire of pardon, blessèd recompense,
Hardly has yet arisen wholly from the grave.

A soul at peace returns not yearning but content,
Equal in daring to the freer element,
Ezekiel-eagle that can stare into the Sun.

Lo! holy boldness, when the mortal war is done:
Heav'n-fledged, unending flight preparing, led no more,
Bright in adoring might, shine forth on golden shore!

107.

Lyrical Response to Sura 102
"Small Kindnesses" and Isaiah

In the name of Allah, the Beneficent, the Merciful.

1. Hast thou observed him who belieth religion?

2. That is he who repelleth the orphan,

3. And urgeth not the feeding of the needy.

4. Ah, woe unto worshippers

5. Who are heedless of their prayer;

6. Who would be seen (at worship)

7. Yet refuse small kindnesses!

Isaiah 58:5. Is it such a fast that I have chosen? a day for a man to afflict his soul? Is it to bow down his head as a bulrush, and to spread sackcloth and ashes under him? wilt thou call this a fast, and an acceptable day to the Lord?

6. Is not this the fast that I have chosen? . . . .

7. . . . . to deal thy bread to the hungry, and that thou bring the poor that are cast out to thy house? when thou seest the naked, that thou cover him; and that thou hide not thyself from thine own flesh?

. . . . .

10. And if thou draw out thy soul to the hungry, and satisfy the afflicted soul; then shall thy light rise in obscurity, and thy darkness be as the noonday. . . .

> Grandly displayed and ostentatious fast,
> And to be more admired at pious prayer —
> External showy focus — a betrayer
> Of what will matter to the man at last.
>
> Ashes and sackcloth, sadness' panoply,
> Leanings that fitter for a bulrush were —
> Heedless, indeed! The starved and poor prefer
> Small kindness, even, to the pride they see.

The orphan from your hearth drive not away,
And let the hungry at your table stay.
Cover the naked. Soul expand, and heart,

Ev'n in the act of giving. The obscure
Turn to the light. Those who their minds immure
In selfhood see but dark — alone, apart.

108.

Lyrical Response to Sura 114 "Mankind"

---

for Katharina Mommsen

In the name of Allah, the Beneficent, the Merciful.

1. Say: I seek refuge in the Lord of mankind,

2. The King of mankind,

3. The God of mankind,

4. From the evil of the sneaking whisperer,

5. Who whispereth in the hearts of mankind,

6. Of the jinn and of mankind.

Ev'n as the Prophet had been sent, a mercy to the worlds,
You have appeared, a morning star, enlightener to me.
How quickening the talisman you have so kindly made!
I say it, not immodest, who have channeled what had come

From sources you had placed nearby, that I might look at these
And power feel, to be transcribed in quiet hours of night.
In Goethe's copied sura see a quest and a reply:
Refuge is gained from whispering, from cunning and from care.

We heard the seeker — how he loud implored! — but where's the gain?
'Tis tidelike intimated in the sounding of the word
"Mankind," five times repeated with a prayer's gentle strength.
To think of humankind united — lo! the secret key.

Allah is Lord of humankind, and yet we know full well
That "Of the jinn and of mankind" there is another bond.
Made of wet clay, we yet are giv'n by Him essential fire,
Jinnlike, that may be used for ill, or (praise the One!) for good.

Five times we hear "mankind" — may these, like to the fingers five
Upon the lucky talisman whose pow'r is Allah's eye,
Be as a holy blessing pledge of brother, sister love,
Growing the early Garden vine of Allah's glowing life.

PART 3

Lyrics on Islam-Related Themes

109.

East-West Poetry: An Introduction

. . . fear of Hellfire, in comparison with fear of being parted from the beloved, is like a drop of water cast into the mightiest ocean. . . .
Dhū'n Nūn, qtd. in Reynold A. Nicholson, The Mystics of Islam *(1914; rpt. ed. Chester Springs PA, 116), qtd. in Annemarie Schimmel,* Mystical Dimensions of Islam *([Chapel Hill: University of North Carolina Press, 1975], 131)*

"Fathers and teachers, I ponder, 'What is hell?' I maintain that it is the suffering of being unable to love."

    (Dostoyevsky, The Brothers Karamazov*)*

Rembrandt's copy of a Mogul miniature, showing the founders of the four great mystical orders. British Museum

    (picture caption, Schimmel, Mystical Dimensions of Islam, *233)*

> Under a tree the turbaned mages take
> Refreshment. They are founders of the four
> Mystical Muslim orders. And they make
>
> In crescent form a rounding. We restore
> An Eden-feeling of a calmed embrace.
> Two birds that perch upon the boughs add more
>
> Emblems of choiring. Thoughtful, every face;
> Focused upon a question all the eyes.
> Friendship has granted here a fourfold grace:
>
> Quiet, convivial, a paradise,
> *Hortus inclusivus*, a love that casts
> All fear away, for now we realize
>
> Sadness can't catch our glad symposiasts.
> Deep-rooted future, branching from our pasts!

110.

Pillars of Islam

As the concentric rings within the eye,
Widen the circles of the duties five:
Statement of faith in Allah, All-alive —
Muhammad, too, loved Prophet; then the high

Delight of prayer, next the fasting in
The month of Ramadan; then, giving alms;
Finally, hajj to Mecca (pilgrim-palms
Come to the mind from times long gone). They win

Favor and grace who with the One begin,
The God who ever broadens our concern.
Five pillars, daily prayers five — we turn

To actions, five the fingers of the Hand
With *ḥamsa,* Eye on palm, that will command
All harm away from heart: we love, we learn.

111.

Mohammed Marmaduke Pickthall

interpreter of the Qur'ân

He saw — and heard, with spirit-ear —
Embraving radiance of the Higher
As of a bright essential fire
That clove the cold at dawn with clear

Uplifted rays like arms outspread,
Such as the Sons of God had raised
At the Creation, when they praised,
With colored stars engarlanded,

One who beyond all works and ways
Of His angelic messengers
Lent strength to all that now concurs
In concord, though by height and haze

Hidden at times from eyes misled
By failings of a mind that's tired
And fading in desire, immired,
A sunken semblance of the dead,

Who may be suddenly returned
To life! Then come!, draw swiftly near —
Translator-singer, ever dear:
We heard you, and the daybreak burned.

112.

After Ten Lyrical Responses to the Qur'an

I had not planned to stand upon the sacred hill
Of Oreb or of Sinai, yet the law came down
Not to refuse, nor, idle, lose the proffered crown,
The heightened mind invested with a deeper will

That whispered, saying, "Write!" and not relenting, till
At length I'd part the clouds that, stifling, loured in frown
Of stern admonishment, pressed on. In prophet-gown
From crystal goblet did I drink, no drop to spill.

The longest revelation I have yet received
Was granted, manifold, to hands that had believed,
And so I felt, my fingers flying over keys

With that unscanted, ample, unexampled ease
Whereby we know the warmth which at our dawn will glow,
I must reply, "I will" when grace would make me grow.

113.

The Muhammadan Rose

on the cover of Annemarie Schimmel's
"And Muhammad Is His Messenger"

The sempiternal souls' amphitheatric rose,
Petals composed of rays within a sea of light,
Greeted the Florentine with solar eagle sight
At Beatrice' behest, for she the poet chose.

Like the Dantescan, two celestial roses grow
On a resplendent and illuminated plant.
Ninety-nine names on each the homage-hierophant
Who twinned Muhammad's, Allah's images made glow.

The flow'rs arise from out a lighter, lower bloom
With heart-forms, this in turn encircled by the ten
Holy ones who were promised Paradise. But when

The Prophet into all the heavens made ascent,
Sarmad said no! He felt they must have humbly bent
To meet the man who mirrored God in mortal room.

114.

Lyrical Response to Schimmel's Muhammad and to Smart and Goethe

For I will consider my cat Jeoffry.
For he is the servant of the Living God, duly and daily serving Him.
For at the first glance of the glory of God in the East he worships in his own way.
For this is done by wreathing his body seven times round with elegant quickness. . . .
For he keeps the Lord's watch in the night against the adversary. . . .
For every house is incomplete without him, and a blessing is lacking in the spirit.

(*Christopher Smart*, Jubilate Agno)

Beside the Lord a cat, caressed,
Abu Hurayra's, purrs.
The holy Prophet, stroking, blest
A friend he yet prefers.

(*J. W. von Goethe*, "Favored Animals")

Muhammad . . . had a special liking for cats. Did he not cut the sleeve from his coat when he had to get up for prayer and yet did not want to disturb the cat that was sleeping on the sleeve? One of his cats even gave birth to kittens on his coat, and special blessings were extended to Abu Huraira's cat, who killed a snake that tried to cheat the Prophet and sting him despite the kindness he had shown it. . . . Remembering the Prophet's fondness for cats, one hadith *claims that "love of cats is part of faith." (Annemarie* Schimmel, And Muhammad Is His Messenger: The Veneration of the Prophet in Islamic Piety *[Chapel Hill and Boston: University of North Carolina Press, 198], 49)*

A cat's an amulet, we can believe,
A talisman, a pledge of blessing. But
It must be loved! Muhammad humbly cut
His coat: the cat was sleeping on the sleeve.

The snake that sought the Healer to bereave
Of life, the sunlike Prophet-eyes to shut
Untimely, died. Watchful, no matter what,
The cat the Master loved would never leave.

My cat who, saved, had been instilled with fears
By an ordeal beneath the city streets,
Reclusive, grieved. Behold! our new cat greets

The moveless hermit. Purring! Ah, the sweets
Of wrestling, fondest caring that endears:
After the contest he would wash her ears.

115.

Tribute to Rumi

---

for Avideh Shashaani

I, from a quiet guidebook, sought a world apart,
To learn Maulana-yearning whirled in rapid trance,
Yet one ecstatic pearl-bright bird in purer dance
Had overruled my reading, offered Allah's art

More deeply piercing than the waking sunray-dart,
Saying, "The twirling round the Holy Countenance
Emblemed in Rumi's tomb in vast green-grand romance
Of Bridegroom and His bride begins within the heart

Where first and last the mausoleum of the saint
That you in Konia viewed, smaragdine majesty
With pillars round below the cone, had praised in paint

The light-born life-seed rising through the morning songs
Wherein we hear the flute that for the reed-bed longs:
Take it into your soul, the holiness of Me."

116.

Maulana Dies and Lives

---

reading Annemarie Schimmel, Rumi's World

A legend-life Maulana Rumi led.
Shams-i Tabrīz and he knew lovers' bond
Like that of Soul and Allah. Overfond,
The son of Rumi, Ala-eddin, fed

A jealous heart — behold! the Friend was dead! —
A desolation that could not be named.
Gloom that would kill the Sun of Hope he blamed...
Union of spirit soothed and comforted:

Shams turned to burning bush, or to the star
Of morning, or the glory of the light.
Silvery sound of goldsmith-hammers bright

Charming the poet's ear at the bazaar
Whirled him about entranced! — and sadness, fright,
Vanished. He'd learned where the Eternal are.

117.

Rumi on Jesus and John the Baptist

---

elaborating a prose paragraph in Annemarie Schimmel, *The Triumphal Sun*,
181

Jesus, continually trusting, smiles,
While John, the melancholic, hides from wrath.
Said John to Jesus: "Too secure, that path!
You laugh. Beware! a cunning lie beguiles."

Jesus replied: "You've simply put aside
The lovingkindness and the grace of God.
You weep in dire dismay — a little odd:
With daybreak, surely dark was well defied?"

One of the saints made bold to ask the Lord
Which of the speakers held the higher station.
The answer came without equivocation:

"The one who's thinking better thoughts of me."
Fear not for love. It wins, not having warred.
Laughter itself will make the spirit free.

118.

Lyrical Response to Rumi and Goethe

---

elaborated from data supplied in Annemarie Schimmel, *Triumphal Sun,* 108;
and see Goethe's quatrain:

If one to Mecca were to ride
Jesus' own donkey, it would not
By this be deepened in its thought
But as a donkey still abide.

  (*J. W. von Goethe*)

> Jesus would ride a donkey. So do we
> As long as loth, untrained, the *nafs* objects,
> Countering discipline, and willfully
> Renouncing heaven, kind constraint neglects.
>
> When you have come to Jesus' own hometown,
> Don't say, "I am a donkey" anymore.
> Jesus went up to God; the donkey, down.
> Donkeys get barley-drunk. For Jesus, pour
>
> No wine that can be made from worldly grape.
> He drinks elixir that to Eden leads.
> See! to his donkey (how the growers gape!)
> He fed that liquor, of the best of steeds
>
> Worthy — Muhammad's flying lightning horse.
> The donkey's sprouting wings! — and up he goes!
> Rising inspired in wind-spurred whirling course,
> Could it be to the King of Kings he rose?
>
> No, it could not, though it was worth a try.
> The soul is whole, the body yet is bound.
> The donkey drops, Messiah yet will fly.
> Jesus — the breeze; the beast is of the ground.

119.

Lyrical Response to Rumi Motifs

For the eyes, heavy-lidded, in wary dismay,
That can barely but wake, and the languorous limbs,
And the muscles benumbed, and the gait gone asway,
And the feet splayed and shaky, the vision that dims,

Every weakness betrays that the sphere called the fourth
Is the one where the donkey of Jesus will halt,
For it cannot go on, though the leader point north
And it's drunk on fermènted sweet barley and malt.

For the mortal is worn, and resources will fail,
And the whip and the prod and the shout and the spurs
And the promise and curse, and the carrot and flail
Cannot salvage the spirit, the body averse.

Though the donkey collapses, Buraq, the bright soul,
Bounding faster than sound, climbing higher than sight,
Will arrive at a hyperheliacal goal
Now awaiting the force of the horses of night!

How the gleams of its hooves mirror, vivid, the spars
From the trail of the rock-streaming meteorites
While elliptical-orbiting wandering stars
Leave in horsetail and spark-raising mane their strange lights.

Be equestrian Àhmad! By Gabriel-aid
With a grateful Recital enswirled in his might
We will copy the Prophet's example who made
A requital of love to the Kindler of Light.

That a being should be, and not nothing at all,
Is the mastering Mystery charging the Mind:
This the Horse, that the Rider! The body may fall,
But the spirit Aurèolar Sabbath shall find.

120.

Dialogue with Rumi

on a story he tells, recounted
in Annemarie Schimmel, *Rumi's World*, 111

When teams in art competed — Byzantine, Chinese —
The latter's training seemed complete; they had been taught
With Manichaean craft (or so the Persian thought).
Would they not win the contest quickly and with ease?

Indeed their splendid mural proved supremely wrought.
But lo! a marvel from Byzantium one sees:
The curtain turned aside, what might more highly please?
Shining, the mirror-marble finer art begot!

Reflected in the breast of ardent worshiper
The form of the beloved will the heart bestir.
But then — will it be mirrored, merely made more bright?

More likely it will stimulate a braver light.
Strive with Aurora! Primal making-rival, move
A dawning word-born world, that morn diviner prove.

121.

Rumi's Hammers

theme from Annemarie Schimmel

Goldsmith-bazaar in Konia: hammer-world!
Patterned, the random rising harmony
Hastened all harm away. Horizon: free.
Friend Salahuddin Zárkub, Rumi, whirled —

New dancing planets. Of the goldsmith we
Know that he couldn't say the seven lines
Of the one crucial sura. Wise divines
Laden with learning — left! For such as he?

Fast-forward to composer Debussy,
In Paris, clapping for the gamelan —
Hammer and block, metallophone and gong:

Transformative coordinated song
According to a novel Javan plan
That planted in the man a legacy.

122.

Mevlana Rumi (1207–1273) and Nasreddin Hodja (1208–1284)

---

based on tales in Annemarie Schimmel, The Triumphal Sun, *259 and Mehmet Ali Birant, compiler,* Nasreddin Hodja *(n.d. Istanbul),* 99

The Persian bard, the comic Turkish priest,
Could they have traded tales — ah, what a spree!
Mevlana tells: a thief had climbed a tree,
The neighbor's fruit to savor — what a feast!

"How dare you take my apples — down, you beast!"
"Ah, but the tree is God's — the fruit is free.
Hey, wait! — what are you doing? Ouch!" "You see?
Behold *God's stick!* Get down! I won't be fleeced!"

A counter-tale: Grim Timur came to town
Set to invade the place, or burn it down.
Hodja said: "Don't *dare enter*, or I know

What I'm prepared to do!" Surprised, defied,
The ugly Sultan angrily replied,
"What?" "Run away, as fast as I can go."

123.

Love-Thoughts and Rumi-Examples

for Katharina Mommsen

part 2 elaborated from Rumi's lines in Annemarie Schimmel's, *As Through a Veil: Mystical Poetry in Islam*, 83–133

> "Nobody's perfect, right?"
> I caught you being perfect seven times tonight.
> "Art copies life. Agree?"
> Lily-ponds seem to emulate Monet, to me.
> Mystical lovers' tunes
> Overturn graves of rulers with their Odin runes.
> Rumi, arrived, will save,
> Opening eye and mind; student to free, and slave:
> . . . . .
> My words are angels' food.
> Angels complain if I am silent: Why be rude?
> I knock upon your gate.
> What use? You're hiding on the highest roof. It's late.
> I read love-stories through:
> I have become a story in my love of you.
> Moth flings himself in fire
> Because a flame appears a window to what's higher.

124.

Annemarumi

Annemarumi, you a laving mantra lent
As on the raving main a waiting lighting went
That with a rainbow made a grateful Noah bow,
A low and roving sound of surf averring now:

"Annemarumi had the will of Allah bent
Blessing the lyres unboundedly in heaven blent
That you and Rumi and the helpful Annemarie
Charming all harm away in trinal harmony

Might now renew the whirling word that, clasping hands,
Rumi and Salahuddin made, which over lands
And oceans would the song and thought of Sufi spread
And bloom the plant and branch the tree and free the dead."

O Allah! Music-boon! May houris by Your might
Let loose with holy force the horses of the night!
Swirl me in spiral worlds, a dervish of the sky,
All-hearing ear, almighty mind, all-lighting eye!

125.

Four Archangels

More terrible and awesome than all angels and spiritual powers, however, is 'Aẓra'il, the angel of death. Of cosmic dimensions, he has 4,000 wings, all beset with tongues and eyes. (Annemarie Schimmel, Islam, *82)*

The third archangel ... is Isrāfīl, who will blow the trumpet that starts the Resurrection. . . . [Some poets] have likened their pen's scratching to Isrāfīl's trumpet because they hoped, or assumed, that their words might awaken their slumbering compatriots and cause a "spiritual resurrection." (Schimmel, Deciphering the Signs of God: A Phenomenological Approach to Islam *[Albany: State University of New York Press, 199], 231)*

Brüder, überm Sternenzelt
Muß ein lieber Vater wohnen.
    (Schiller, "An die Freude")

And saints will aid if men will call,
For the blue sky bends over all.
    (Coleridge, "Christabel")

Emerald-wingèd Michael, nourisher,
And Gabriel, the herald of a birth
To Mary and awakener of earth,
Who would the Mercy of the World bestir,

Helping the Prophet at the Cave Recital —
Whose color, like Mevlana's dome, is green,
The hope of Eden — aid me, souls serene,
To summon up what virtue will be vital.

Four thousand wings, beset with tongues and eyes
Aspiring writer-minds might well advise
To muster love, that will alone arise.

My pen a trumpet, let a muezzin-call
Move awe-filled through the starry blue-roofed hall
Past minaret and tent: bend over all!

126.

Rabi'a of Basra (d. 801)

reworking of a prose anecdote
cited in Annemarie Schimmel's
"Islam: An Introduction" 104–5

In Basra she'd been carrying
Bucket and torch. We asked her why.
"Pour water into hell! On high
Set fire to paradise! And fling

The veils away! Dispel the night:
Don't praise the Lord in fear of hell
Or heaven-hope. They worship well
Who love His beauty." Lofty, right,

And wise! For in similitudes
Allah the Pedagogue alludes
To water holes and desert fire.

Yet ardor's part of high desire;
Wild water — life, yet death as well.
Widen your mind past heaven, hell...

127.

To Our Mentor, Ebusu'ud

---

recalling Goethe's "Fetwa" — for Katharina Mommsen

A man had feared he would be swiftly headed for
A fiery time in Iblis. Thoughts the good abhor
He had absorbed in reading... Do they not disclose

A hot postmortal prospect waiting there for those
Who may peruse the lines whereinto writers pour
Dire cornucopias of soul-aborting lore?

Quoth Ebusu'ud: 'Tis the wiser mind that knows
Venom from theriac, and freely, gladly goes
Quickly to what the willing spirit will restore.
What oversteps the limit — this regard no more.

In humble human scripture love-in-oneness grows
To be of widest light the kernel and the core.
Mutual mirrors are the foes in "noble" war.
It is to praise and raise a paean we arose.

128.

Buraq

See here the speed wherewith the speech of Allah wrought
Works lightning-livelier than labor-laden thought!
Good reason that the cleaving flame-blade's called a tongue
Extending through the waving air-heat, proud outflung.

Speaking in tongues that are mosaic flames outflown,
Bird-bush whose words are unconsumed, in blest breath blown,
Flowering, spread symmetric petals flaring red
Send out at every hour th' ineffable re-said.

Why is Buraq the high and guiding metaphor
Of human thought and song and awe-born storm that pour
From out the soul and heart and mind and mouth and more?

Swifter than sound and sight, electron-energies'
Urging, while yet traversing times, eternities,
Creation replicating — His, our hymnodies.

129.

Al-Buraq

---

for Katharina Mommsen

Goethe und der Islàm for me is Al-Buraq.
All should be taught about that steed. (Bucephalus
That Alexander tamed can't mean so much to us,
Though Pegasean, too.) It brought Muhammad back

After a dreamlike journey to Jerusalem
From Mecca, at the speed of light. For as the name
Of the bright-blinding creature tells, it well might claim
To be no less than *Lightning*. Very like to them —

Goethe, and Gottfried Herder, and the *hen kai pan*
Comrade Baruch, or Benedictus, and the man
(Not god) Muhammad, who through seven heavens went —

The reader of your book, aroused with ardor for
The western mental blendings with Islamic lore,
Will rise enlightened, *ein Gesandter*, heaven-sent.

130.

Persian

I came like water, and like wind I go,
Or as a cloud crossing the light, a shade
Cast on the green, a shadow that I made,
Forming whatever pattern I might throw.

I came like water, and like wind I go.
Edward FitzGerald in his journey played
The role of Omar, in a robe arrayed
That *Shah-Namàh* had shown him how to sew.

I came like water, and like wind I go.
The lives of Rustum and of Sohrab, weighed
By Arnold, and Zhukovsky, were portrayed
Flying, a cloud on high, and then brought low.

They flee me now that loved me. All things flow.
I came like water, and like wind I go.

131.

The Qur'an

Several hundred pages' worth of wait
Before the Castle never would avail —
Grey, clammy walls and ever-fastened gate —
For K. was fated, as he knew, to fail.

What of the nearby Palace? Rumors of
A feast within — music, and painting — wares
Lavished by Eastern caravans... Above —
Echoes? Of tales, and poetries, and prayers...

Why doesn't anybody try the door?
Why do the somber walkers look away?
So grim — as if they're marching off to war!

One said he'd heard the building used to be
Locked. "Do you hope to find the key some day?"
"No one had ever hinted it to me."

132.

Allah and Buddha

---

reading Chödrön, Start Where You Are *with*
K. *Mommsen,* Goethe und der Islam

Open your heart up wholly to what's there.
The will of Allah and our Buddha nature:
The same acceptance, varied nomenclature.
Set free an ego that is carking care.

Passion, aggression, ignorance are where
Poison can turn into a healing potion.
They are the busy mind's projective motion:
Touch them and gently label. Open air

Will ventilate them, *lojong* logic dare
Give little cakes not only to protectors
But to the *dön,* unreasoned spurts, correctors

Of our unmindfulness. Each upstart flare
Attended to and entered, we're aware
Detectors, unjudgmental, not rejectors.

133.

West-East Sonnet for Katharina Mommsen

White, clustered roses, opulent, like peonies;
Yellow and red, bold birds of paradise in bloom —
Linear, pointed, angled lightning-bolts — illume
In the dim twilight blue a life one seldom sees.

Hafiz would be at home on Palo Alto Ave.
To California flow'rs add Carolina birds —
Cardinal, caliph-stork — in wide-eyed Schlayer-words:
Many the languages of wonder that we have,

Lauding in gloom and gladness what the world affirms.
Goethe und der Islàm: the symbol-lore the same.
Creatures of earth and air add each another name

To the unnumbered body, shape, and color terms
Glossing each Allah-word with changed illumination.
He makes again each day the dawn of the Creation.

134.

It Came to Me on Waking

It came to me on waking. Coffee not yet done,
I turned to the Qur'an to write a morning hymn,
Wanting to float in air of imagery, to swim
In flood-association of the songs that, spun

Out of the spider-night, by dewy light of dawn
Reflect in spectral gleaming tones the photic dance
Of quick reflections that on web-spread texture glance
With sparkling, snow-pure globes enlightening the lawn.

O Maker of the Daybreak! You it is who "cleave"
The unlike worlds apart, yet bring them back again
To "cleave" together! So, in double-meaning word

A love-and-stress, a twofold message, may be heard.
Our June is janual. Each moment is a door,
Exit and entrance, telling what our breath is for.

135.

Found on My Lawn This Morning

I look with a pleasurable surprise:
A peacock plume in a Kóran lies.

  (J. W. von Goethe, "Ich seh' mit Staunen und Vergnügen")

Black pennon trapped amid the grass
And shining with its native oil
In cross-hatch patterns, well-besprent
    With raindrops large and small,

Betokening a far-off mass
Of winds that blust'ring, rage and roil,
Came as a little symbol sent:
    Storms, pounding, that appall

And far away their growl make heard,
In swirling currents to deflect
The thrust of crows, though sentry-led,
    This tiny trophy gained.

I love the raven, omen-bird
Of Odin. Crows would aid, protect
Abel, and Cain was comforted,
    Though ever after pained,

When they arrived (the Kóran tells)
To show how men are laid to rest,
Buried in peace. We learn to live
    With dying in the heart.

Black feather! You no mourning bells
Tolled but attained a greening nest
And are a friend to me, to give
    Your dark and perfect art.

136.

Typos, Begone!

The jinns are of essential fire,
And I of only wet clay altered.
I saw that when my hand had faltered
In characters of my desire

They'd vainly tried, with crafty ire,
By tiny items (for they paltered,
Lacking all hope to hold me haltered)
To quiet one of Allah's choir.

O spirit that shall never die
Within the flying fingers till
It be the time His holy will

Had set, may I, yet fierier,
Conquer the clay with striving stir
By image bright as Allah's eye!

137.

For Michael Engelhard

a grateful embrace

Upon a wave in bliss I rode
While writing through the night and day
My Dìvan: fire the conquered clay
Enlivened till my fingers glowed:

Streaming, each line I wrote; they flowed
Sun-heart-made sky-vein, ardent ray
That shone, infinities away
On Lote-Tree, Garden of Abode.

How bright we gleam! when horses of
The night are loosed, Buraq in love
Bathed in a balm that heals in light!

O saint Rabi'a, benedight,
Who comest from the dusk champaign
Lucent on ways that may not wane!

138.

For My Newest Friend, Thomas Ogger

I hope, in Germany, we'll speak at length
Together of the spirit you instill
In these your writings, deep their tranquil strength.

Baba Tahir and Hallaj, Francis fill
(As Yunus, Rumi, Juan and Scheffler do)
The soul with mountain streams that overspill

Blending the red of heart-love with the blue
Breadth of the boundless. For the Jujube Tree
Borders the Garden of Abode, yet you

And I are there, for never galaxy
Exploded that we don't today explore
Simply in living through the unity

Of star and seed and wave and light. That lore
To sing is why we're born, it's what we're for.

139.

Hegel's Hafiz

... a free, happy depth of feeling is characteristic of [...] especially the Mohammedan Persians, who openly and cheerfully sacrifice their entire selves to God and to everything praiseworthy, yet in this sacrifice they do precisely retain the free substantiality which they can perceive even in relation to the surrounding world. So we see in the glow of passion the most widespread bliss and parrhesia of feeling through which, in the inexhaustible wealth of brilliant and splendid images, there resounds the steady note of joy, beauty, and good fortune. In the poems of Hafiz ... even in grief he remains just as carefree as he is in good fortune. So, e.g., he says once: "Out of thanks that the presence of thy friend enlightens thee, in woe burn like the candle and be satisfied."

The candle teaches us to laugh and cry; through the flame it laughs in cheerful splendour, while at the same time it melts away in hot tears; in its burning it spreads cheerful splendour. This is the general character of this whole poetry.

(G. W. F. Hegel, Aesthetics: Lectures on Fine Art,
tr. T. M. Knox [Oxford: Clarendon Press, 1988] I.369)

I am a candle, having learned of height from trees
And sharing in my flame the colors of their fall.
I have a many-circled shining eye that frees

An allegory of the passing time of all
By seeing in my mirror-fire a glory grow.
Thankful in being lighted, I am lighter. Tall

Are they who laugh and cry and hymn and sigh and glow.
Parrhesial feeling! — deep, for breathing is belief.
Heat is a leaf, a life, a sand-grain atom. So

We rise above our waxen woe, our molten grief,
Encompassed by the light spread by the spirit eye,
The sun, the dreaming Pleiades, their beauty brief,

The light in bloody sky blazoning forth His name
No more subdued than I, hued in a loving flame.

140.

Rumi and Hegel

Although [Rumi] was so fond of mystical dance that he even gave correct legal decisions (fātvā) during his whirling dance, he led an extremely ascetic life.... (Annemarie Schimmel, The Triumphal Sun, *28)*

The breeze, again, is a fitting symbol of the life-giving breath of the Beloved: the twigs and branches become intoxicated and dance, touched by the wind, stamping their feet on the tomb of January, and clapping their hands. Even more: the spring breeze becomes visible in the rosebeds and sweet herbs: invisible waves of roses hidden in the breeze need the medium of the earth to become visible to the human eye, just as man's qualities must be revealed by outward means, be it speech, fighting, or peace-making. (Schimmel, 86)

But it was the Ghaselen *that deeply influenced the German reading public. Through these verses Hegel became acquainted with "the excellent Rumi" who seemed to constitute for him a perfect model of pantheistic thought. (Schimmel, 391)*

The True is thus the Bacchanalian revel in which no member is not drunk; and yet because each member collapses as soon as he drops out, the revel is just as much transparent and simple repose. (Hegel, Phenomenology of Mind*)*

> Move to the music, Hegel, in your Sufi-wool!
> Enter the revel where no member is not drunk!
> Imbibe sweet heaven-wine, in sea of Eden sunk,
> Feeling the breezes which in spring-arising pull
>
> To spry embodiment the waves invisible
> That in the dance of history will be revealed,
> And on the tomb of gloomy January sealed,
> Stamp with a fevered heat, of jinn-like furor full!
>
> O Bacchanalian Hegel, teller of the True!
> Rumi awakes the youthful Sufi-wail in you!
> The rosebud and the herb, the sapling twig and branch
>
> Hasten the blood-flow that the winter chill would stanch:
> Hail to Mevlana, who with dervish whirl enticed
> Leavening levity of geyser, yeast, and Geist!

Index

flesh, 131, 151
flies, 134, 138
flight, 95, 133
flood, 83, 183
flow, 179
flower, 31, 63, 161, 177, 182
fluid, 83
flute, 16, 46, 68, 96, 108, 119, 164
fly, xiv, 108, 133, 137
foe, 105, 113, 140, 176
food, 80, 81
force, 173
forgive, xvi, xx, 8, 23, 24, 39, 45, 53,
    59, 64, 72, 116, 123, 150
fount, 48, 49, 96
fountain, 33, 83, 131
Francis of Assisi, St., 187
free, 106, 166, 172, 173, 181, 188
freedom, xv, 48, 79, 94, 124
friend, 144, 150
fruit, 21, 22, 29, 31, 32, 60, 80, 81, 97,
    98, 142, 171
furnace, xiii
future, 74, 157

— G —

Gabriel, xvii, xviii, 20, 29, 34, 43, 86,
    94, 95, 125, 126, 168, 174
Gaea, 56
gain, 127
garden, xii, xix, 8, 15, 19, 28, 48, 53,
    57, 60, 64, 65, 66, 68, 70, 72, 80,
    84, 114, 120, 128, 144, 154, 186,
    187
garment, 128
gate, 27, 44, 114, 133, 134, 172
Geist, 189
generous, 36, 97
Genesis, xii, 60
Gihon, 60
giving, 152
gladness, 182
gloom, 182, 189

glory, 96, 100, 115
goal, 127
goblet, 84, 144, 160
God, xxvii, 26, 34, 36, 40, 41, 46, 48,
    61, 77, 86, 100, 103, 111, 112, 114,
    116, 118, 119, 120, 122, 123, 126,
    127, 128, 135, 136, 137, 143, 146,
    150, 153, 158, 161, 162, 166, 167,
    171, 188
Goethe, J. W. von, xxii, xxiii, xxv,
    xxviii, 103, 105, 107, 109, 132, 135,
    137, 139, 144, 153, 162, 167, 176,
    178, 181, 182, 184
goldsmith, 165, 170
good, xvi, 27, 35, 43, 45, 46, 47, 53,
    64, 82, 146
Gospel, xii, xvi, 12, 14, 20, 62, 120
grace, 24, 26, 36, 41, 61, 70, 84, 86,
    89, 122, 123, 136, 139, 140, 157,
    158, 160, 166
gracious, 36
grain, xvi, 6, 15, 21, 109
grape, 32, 33
grass, 15
gratitude, 123, 131, 147
grave, 55, 96, 150
greed, 31, 56, 72, 97
green, 174, 179, 184
grief, 188
ground, 49, 128, 167
grow, 160
guardian, 83
guide, xxiii, 142

— H —

hadith, xvii, xix, xxv, 34, 91, 125, 162
Hafiz, xxix, 182, 188
hajj, 158
Halima, 118
Hallaj, xix, xxix, 20, 112, 187
Haman, 48
hammer, 165, 170
hamsa, xvii, 158

~ 195 ~

127, 128, 141, 142, 166, 167, 168
jeweled, 138
Jewish, xiii
jinn, xiv, xvi, xvii, xxiii, xxvii, 23, 29,
    30, 45, 46, 47, 49, 53, 59, 65, 68,
    71, 82, 83, 100, 112, 124, 130, 143,
    146, 153, 154, 185, 189
John the Baptist, xxi, 166
joke, 130
Jonah, xv, 77
Jordan, 127
Joseph, xiii, xxi, 4, 26, 121, 123
journey, 82, 127, 135, 178
joy, 106, 123, 146
Juan (St. John of the Cross), 187
Judaism, xii, xvii
judgment, xvii, 1, 103
jujube, 187
justice, 149

— K —

K. (in Kafka), 180
Kant, Immanuel, 52
key, 180
Khadija, 38
Khayyám, Omar, xx
kill, 45, 137
kind, 23, 24, 36, 71, 81, 88, 131, 137,
    146, 151, 162, 167
kindness, 166
king, 51, 54, 57, 71, 79, 100, 117, 131,
    145, 153, 167
kingdom, 51
knife, 90
knots, 99
knowledge, 111
Konia, xx, 141, 164, 170
Koran, xxv, 94, 111, 115, 120, 123,
    125, 129, 141, 144, 146, 184

— L —

labor, 95, 142, 149

lamp, 41, 43
land, 85, 105, 107, 109, 139
language, 64, 182
laugh, 130, 132, 166, 188
law, 48, 52, 55, 160
leaf, 188
Lessing, Gotthold Ephraim, xxviii
liberty, 110
life, xvi, 13, 25, 30, 33, 36, 40, 41, 43,
    46, 48, 56, 57, 58, 72, 73, 74, 82,
    83, 92, 94, 96, 97, 99, 100, 106,
    108, 111, 117, 120, 124, 134, 136,
    146, 154, 159, 164, 172, 175, 182,
    188, 189
light, xii, xvii, xxvii, 6, 12, 14, 34, 36,
    41, 43, 46, 48, 49, 50, 57, 62, 78,
    89, 90, 97, 98, 99, 103, 105, 107,
    110, 111, 123, 125, 128, 130, 131,
    151, 152, 161, 165, 168, 169, 173,
    176, 178, 179, 183, 186, 187, 188
lightning, xix, xxv, 29, 34, 44, 45, 94,
    115, 126, 146, 167, 177, 182
lily, xxi, 120, 128
live, 44, 59, 184
live, 109
live, 111
lojong, 181
loneliness, 95
Lord, 7, 8, 26, 27, 29, 32, 35, 36, 39,
    45, 46, 49, 51, 52, 53, 54, 60, 61,
    64, 68, 72, 74, 76, 77, 80, 88, 92,
    94, 95, 98, 99, 100, 104, 115, 116,
    127, 134, 148, 150, 151, 154, 162,
    166, 175
losers, 74
lote tree, xix, 29, 65, 66, 186
    jujube tree, xix
love, xx, xxi, 5, 8, 13, 15, 18, 22, 23,
    31, 41, 46, 56, 57, 58, 59, 63, 86,
    89, 91, 97, 100, 106, 114, 115, 123,
    125, 129, 134, 135, 141, 142, 146,
    154, 157, 158, 166, 168, 172, 174,
    176, 179, 183, 186, 188

Sheba, 15
Shelley, Percy Bysshe, xxviii, 1
shelter, 106
ship, xiv, 55, 139, 140
shirt, xxi, 121, 122
sigh, 147
sight, 50, 61, 177
Silesius, Angelus, xxix
similitude, xii, xiv, 10, 29, 31, 41, 60,
    87, 133, 175
simoom, 88, 114
sin, xx, 150
Sinai, 160
singer, 159
sirocco, 88, 114
sixty-six, xxvii
sky, 43, 46, 56, 57, 73, 86, 91, 96, 105,
    106, 131, 136, 139, 149, 173, 174,
    186, 188
slave, 86, 172
slumber, 25
Smart, Christopher, xx, 162
smoke, 56, 59
snake, 162
snow, 183
Sohrab, 179
soil, 121
solace, 90, 92
solar, 87, 103, 106, 118, 146
solitude, 57, 128
Solomon, xiv, 12, 46, 49
son, 37, 98
song, 83, 144, 164, 170, 173, 177, 183
Song of Solomon, 15
Sons of God, 100, 159
sorrow, 104, 127
soul, 35, 38, 44, 67, 71, 73, 82, 87, 89,
    96, 105, 114, 116, 119, 120, 121,
    123, 127, 128, 130, 131, 137, 150,
    151, 152, 161, 164, 165, 168, 174,
    176, 177
sound, 177
Southern, 105, 107

spear, 108
speech, 177, 189
speed, 177, 178
sperm, 94
spheres, 146
spider, xiv, xix, xxi, 137, 183
Spinoza, Baruch/Benedictus, 178
spirit, 14, 83, 87, 94, 95, 98, 99, 100,
    108, 115, 119, 121, 124, 128, 141,
    142, 146, 159, 162, 165, 166, 168,
    174, 176, 185, 187, 188
spring, 50, 51, 61, 70, 71, 84, 120, 144,
    148, 189
St. Francis, xxix
St. John of the Cross, xxix
staff, 45
star, xvii, xxiii, xxiv, 6, 12, 25, 35, 41,
    43, 52, 65, 69, 73, 82, 87, 109, 136,
    146, 153, 159, 165, 168, 174, 187
stealth, 97
steed, 94, 125, 167
stillness, 109
sting, 162
stories, 172
stork, 182
storm, 15, 21, 49, 53, 68, 177, 184
straight path, 103, 105, 107
stream, 49, 61, 122
strength, 87, 159, 187
stress, 134
strife, 25, 134
struggle, 25
suffer, 56, 89, 116, 127, 146
Sufi, xx, xxix, 104, 115, 116, 146, 150,
    173, 189
Sultan, 171
summoner, 43
sun, 6, 9, 11, 12, 15, 28, 36, 40, 41, 46,
    50, 51, 53, 56, 59, 68, 70, 80, 81,
    82, 83, 87, 89, 100, 103, 105, 106,
    108, 109, 121, 123, 129, 132, 141,
    142, 146, 150, 162, 164, 165, 166,
    167, 171, 186, 189